CHRISTIA[
DELVERAI
BOOK 3

CW00501740

"Walking
In
Victory"

**PART THREE OF A TEACHING
MANUAL ON CASTING OUT DEMONS
FOR CHRISTIAN SOLDIERS**

PETER HOBSON

First Edition   1988
Second Edition   1997

Copyright © 1988

The author (Peter Hobson) takes full and sole moral and legal responsibility before God and man for all the material presented in this publication, and no other person, notwithstanding other persons named in this publication.

The translation of Bible passages are usually the author's unless indicated otherwise.

National Library of Australia I.S.B.N.
Christian Deliverance Series 0 947252 00 2 (Set)
Book 3 "Walking in Victory" 0 947252 03 7

Printed in Sri Lanka by New Life Literature (Pvt) Ltd.,
                         Spur Road 4, I.P.Z.
                         Katunayake
                         Sri Lanka

CONTENTS

BOOK 3: "WALKING IN VICTORY"

INTRODUCTION

CHAPTER 7:   THE BATTLE IS WON BUT THE WAR IS NOT OVER

CHAPTER 8: OPPOSITION   47

INTRODUCTION

This book had to be written. It can save you a great deal of heart-ache and disappointment. How? Because it is so easy for the enemy to rob God's people of the Victory they have prayed and fought for, during the very last round of a fight, simply because of MISUNDERSTANDING. We aim to remove misunderstanding with God's truth!

There are two ways to learn – the "easy" way and the hard way. I decided about ten years ago I was sick of learning the hard way, which was basically trusting in the Lord through my own fleshly understanding and doing what seemed right to ME. This is the exact opposite of Proverbs 3:5.

"Trust in the LORD with ALL your heart and do NOT lean on your own understanding".

Verlie and I have learned from others. We have learned from history, from the Reformation, the Wesleyan Revival, theological lecturers and some charismatic leaders but most of all we have been driven back into the Word of God, time and time again, to be taught by the Holy Spirit. We would like to spare you the hard way, the slow way, so this series has been written that you might have recourse, in a few pages, to what the good Lord has taught us over 24 years in Deliverance Ministry. We are a MINISTRY. It is not my purpose, nor the purpose of Full Salvation Fellowship to build a new Church or ANY form of Empire, but to help RENEW ANY CHURCH, ANYWHERE in the World.

Doors have already opened in the Philippines, India and Africa. Praise the Lord! It does not matter to us whether a local church is traditional or charismatic and into the Renewal movement, although Renewal churches will have an enormous head-start in the current move of the Holy Spirit. Our calling and Vision is to help any Pastor or Church begin to prepare their people of God for the Wedding Feast, and we will do anything within our power and commission from the Lord to help YOU, that is, to help you get Deliverance and Restoration meetings going for your precious people.

This *may* cause you some change of policy and direction as the larger Vision of the mind of Christ is revealed to you, but what good is any policy if it does not keep up with the leading of the Holy Spirit? It may be necessary for your church leaders to CRUCIFY the lusts of the flesh regarding their desire for church growth. Many programs seeking to do this may be commendable but if our MOTIVES are polluted with empire-building ambitions of personal glory they can never succeed in the long term. **Juan Carlos Ortiz** once described this Church syndrome as "growing FAT, not strong".

Alternatively, a RESTORATION program for the people of God in your care will "automatically" prosper because this is what the true, full-on, elect people of God everywhere have unknowingly been waiting for, and of course, it will have the Lord's blessing. It will mean warfare BUT the battles will be decided in your favour because you are ministering HIS URGENT will for the End-Time.

It is important to remind ourselves that the race we run as Christians during this earthly pilgrimage is:

(i)   not a sprint but a long distance endurance race;

(ii) requires a level of commitment to the Lord that

truly accepts NO reservations, for all things about us are exposed by the inner searching of ourselves by His Holy Spirit, sooner or later;

(iii) based on the truth that obedience is better than sacrifice. We remain totally convinced that **the Lord's directions to born again Christians to cleanse themselves is a command**, not an option, according to the Word of God (2 Cor. 3:18, 7:1, James 4:8, 2 Tim. 2:21-22, 1 John 3:2-3, Dan. 12:10 - see Appendix J).

It follows from this that a very large proportion of the Body of Christ is living in disobedience. Is it any wonder that there is so much division and defeat, even amongst those who understand "victory-living" in theory?

I am compelled to say that local Churches which OBEY and prepare their people for the Bridegroom's coming by personal deliverance through a serious Restoration program will not only survive the coming seasons of world distress but will prosper. Likewise Churches which continue to seek and fulfill a vision of their own making - no matter how big, powerful and successful they have been - and continue to ignore the PRIOR WILL OF CHRIST in this matter will eventually stumble and crumble, and great will be the fall. *"Except the Lord build the house, those who build it labour in vain"* (Ps. 127:1).

Dear Pastors and leaders of God's people, it is a matter of *PREPARE THEM, OR LOSE THEM* to some other Pastor who is willing to do, in the Name and power of the Great Shepherd of the Sheep, what you are NOT willing to do. The direction we take in this matter is critical to aligning us with the wise or foolish virgins, the true or the harlot church.

You may not like what I am saying but I beseech you to consider it and bring it before the Throne. Pastors! Now is the time! Now is the Hour to prepare your people, by means of a deep, inner cleansing with the deliverance FIRE of the Holy Spirit.

I beg you not to be too proud to ask for help, nor to harden your hearts as the people of God did in the wilderness, but to make your election sure (2 Peter 1:10-11). So then brethren, let us put to death all the bickering over traditional points of peripheral doctrine, and jealousy over lost and stolen sheep; let us stir up our minds and get moving into a Full Salvation, that is, the RESTORATION of individual Christians, and thereby make the TRUE Bride ready for the Wedding.

And now, to refresh your memory, here are the headings of the subject matter already presented in Books 1 and 2:

BOOK 1: "MAKE YOURSELVES READY"

CHAPTER 1. UNDERSTANDING THE PROBLEM
1.   Clarifying of Terms
      (i)   Antichrist
      (ii)   Exorcism
      (iii)   Deliverance
      (iv)   Spirit
      (v)   Manifestation
      (vi)   Demonisation
      (vi)   Can a Christian be demonised?
      (vii)   Filled with the Spirit
2.   The Widespread Need and Scope of the Ministry
3.   The Occult Area

CHAPTER 2. THE CHRISTIAN SOLUTION
1.   Preaching

CHAPTER 7

THE BATTLE IS WON
BUT THE WAR IS NOT OVER

7.1   BATTLE TACTICS OF THE ENEMY

We have indicated in chapters one, five and six that most healing and deliverance is progressive for a variety of reasons and some folk make dramatic progress from the beginning with hardly any obstacles. They not only get better and know it, but they feel it too. Others are getting better but feel worse for a season. Ignorance at this point of how to interpret our SYMPTOMS can be very damaging to one's own morale and to the Kingdom of God. It's rather like going to the doctor. Sometimes medicine achieves immediate improvement in a patient, but at other times, depending on the affliction, severe diarrhoea or septic poisoning may result for a season until the tide of battle turns and the patient makes a good recovery. The medicine may not only be very distasteful but may make one's condition feel terrible, however we usually proceed on the basis that the doctor knows best. We never win a battle by running away.

If you can trust your doctor in such circumstances, how much more should you trust God's Word for deliverance, knowing that the removal of SPIRITUAL muck is the desired result. It is not unusual for Christians to come rushing up and plead for deliverance from demons, giving the appearance of single-mindedness in wanting everything that God has for them (and they genuinely do), but then, as they make a start and the Holy Spirit searches their heart and soul, they begin to glimpse and FEEL for themselves, in their emotions and bodies, the true situation and what

God sees in them. The whole truth is always MORE than we suspect and sometimes it is not easy to accept. The powers of darkness and their hidden kingdoms will be alarmed at the exposure - at the searching of the Spirit - and they will be stirred up to react. THEY WILL DO EVERY-THING THEY KNOW to dissuade the sufferer from proceeding with the ministry of deliverance by faith, and THE CLOSER TO THE HEART OF THE PROBLEM THE MINISTRY TOUCHES, THE GREATER WILL BE THE PRESSURE from the powers of darkness to stop! Watch out for all sorts of obstacles - new romances - sick relatives - extra domestic burdens - interstate trips etc. Satan will concede the child of God some very attractive benefits in order that his kingdom in the human soul shall remain unmolested and unchallenged. People with "strong personalities" (i.e. dominating people) are particularly prone to change their minds suddenly and run away - no prizes for knowing why.

Derek Prince says in his cassette tape message **"Witch-craft, the Public Enemy Number One"** that the characteristic of "domination is evil and very often Witchcraft" and he is right. *Domination and being strong-willed in the worldly sense is unclean,* and Christians certainly need to be broken of these bondages. The Word of God says that when we are weak then we are strong (2 Cor. 12:10) meaning that when we are *yielded* to the will of God (not ours) then His strength fills us, for He chooses the weak to shame the strong (1 Cor. 1:27). Many dominating people have come to us for Christ's deliverance in the past, but very few have stayed long enough to get any real measure of blessing. Why? Firstly, they want to dictate to you how you should minister to them and secondly, when that fails, they try to tell you how you should minister to others. Needless to say, if you give way to either pressure, the ministry then comes under the control of unclean spirits and ends in futility and disarray.

One can understand therefore that the greatest obstacle to the deliverance of dominating people, is their own inability to submit themselves to another, to become a servant instead of a master, because as soon as the Holy Spirit begins to overcome the unclean, the person will be strongly tempted to run away from the ministry. The ironic side of the situation is that they often continue to refer other needy people to the ministry, while staying away themselves. Such is the spiritual "mixture" of the Holy Spirit and the witchcraft kingdom within the soul that they will continue to recognise the worth of the ministry of deliverance and dominate others to receive it but seem unable to apply their own advice to themselves.

Many such people mean well, of course. They may have seen **Bill Subritsky** in action or read of **Derek Prince's** methods and want the same, but that is to fail to understand the uniqueness of every sufferer and the consequential leading of the Spirit upon every minister[1]. If they cannot trust you and the ministry of the Lord through you, they would be better off finding a ministry they CAN trust, if they can bring themselves to trust ANY minister. The Macedonians were blessed because they trusted the Lord FIRST *and also Paul and his fellow apostles,* by the will of God (2 Cor. 8:5). Trusting the minister is especially necessary in deliverance work, which ministers to the soulish area.

There is no need for running away if the sufferer truly trusts the Lord Jesus *and* the person ministering Jesus' deliverance, for the Lord has promised in His Word that we shall not be tested beyond our ability to withstand the testing (1 Cor. 10:13) – Praise the Lord!

---

[1] "Minister" here and throughout means "servant" (of the Lord) and not necessarily an ordained professional clergyman.

Plainly, any **kingdom of satan** (within a soul that has asked for deliverance) is going to endeavour to close ranks and fight against the **Kingdom of God** within the same person. **Fear** spirits may be thrown into the front line in order to make the subject feel so fearful that they will never return again for continuing ministry. Or it may be spirits of **doubt** or **unbelief,** so that in spite of all the evidence of effective ministry and the testimony of many witnesses, the subject finds it extremely difficult to believe what is happening to him and that he is progressing. **Unbelief** is a powerful weapon in snuffing out a victorious work - if it is permitted. Another campaign method common to ruling-class unclean spirits, is to pour in reserves of **confusion.** In this way the subject doesn't know what to think and is less than helpful to those endeavouring to minister. Again the plan is to bring the subject into despair and a sense of hopelessness so that the battle will be broken off and the powers of darkness continue, without threat, their mission in the life of the Christian, attempting to nullify all the good intentions, and render powerless and ineffective any real attempt to serve Christ. You will notice that the three spirits nominated above, fear, unbelief and confusion, are all in the **MIND control** area so watch out for others such as **intellectualism** under this ruler.

These are just some possibilities and things may even "improve" for the sufferer for a season if they quit, as the battle simmers down, but in the long term quitters don't win.

(i)   THE DELIVERANCE CYCLE

If sufferers can understand the battle lines which are drawn up by the Holy Spirit they will probably press on to victory. If they fail to understand these battle lines they will probably misinterpret their symptoms and feelings, get discouraged and pull back, retreating in confusion and disappointment.

Let me explain more fully. We have already said something about the battle tactics of the enemy and how he throws in his troops of fear, confusion and unbelief, very often using relatives and close Christian friends; but while he is doing that, the Holy Spirit is also waging war on our behalf, and, praise the Lord, He has promised us victory in the Word of God if we will only hold the Faith Position and TRUST His promises until victory is achieved. The sequence of events for those receiving regular deliverance ministry is something like this:

1. You receive deliverance ministry because of the promise of God and your obedience to His Word (see Appendix J).

2. The battle flares up and very quickly *the enemy puts his finger on your weaknesses* and *tests out* your Godly conviction to be cleansed and free; consequently you may not feel so good or think too clearly, because of fear, unbelief, confusion etc.

3. You may manifest OBVIOUSLY or VISIBLY (usually physically) your unclean nature as the unclean spirit *surfaces* just prior to exit (e.g. withdrawal symptoms for coffee or heavier addictions). You feel *terrible,* somewhere between *irritable* and *hateful.*

4. As you *resist* the lusts of the enemy within (James 4:6-8), the unclean spirit is *forced to depart* and you experience release, sometimes without even realising it. You feel yourself again.

5. You may get a short season of *blessing* and *respite*

before the Holy Spirit *continues* this warfare within you and searches out the next enemy for eviction.

The cycle looks something like this:

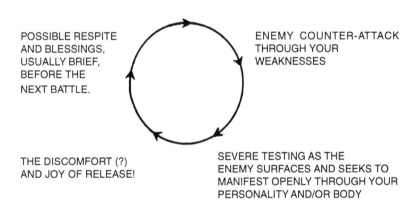

DELIVERANCE MINISTRY BEGINS

POSSIBLE RESPITE AND BLESSINGS, USUALLY BRIEF, BEFORE THE NEXT BATTLE.

ENEMY COUNTER-ATTACK THROUGH YOUR WEAKNESSES

THE DISCOMFORT (?) AND JOY OF RELEASE!

SEVERE TESTING AS THE ENEMY SURFACES AND SEEKS TO MANIFEST OPENLY THROUGH YOUR PERSONALITY AND/OR BODY

Beginning at the top, follow the ministry cycle around in a clockwise direction, and remember, if you can hold the faith position and follow the counselling and teaching you will receive right through to release, then you have won that battle. If you cannot, then you lose that battle. Nobody else on this earth can win or lose your battles for you, except yourself. But of course the Lord has guaranteed you victory through the Cross of Christ Jesus, IF you want it badly enough and can trust His Word when the battle is hottest.

Are you prepared to take your victories in the Name of your Saviour and Lord?

Let me encourage you by saying that for many sufferers it is not as hard as It sounds, but you should be forewarned so that when your testing time comes you will understand what is happening in your soulish area - and WIN! I trust you can now say with Paul that you are not ignorant of satan's designs (2 Cor. 2:11) as far as the reactions of your own soul are concerned, but we will say more about this whole subject later in chapter 8.1 under the heading **"Opposition within Themselves."** The thing to remember is that the god of this world will use all the spiritual agencies available to him in order to pressure the sufferer to discontinue ministry. Thus it becomes vital in post-deliverance counselling to remove the spiritual blindness of the sufferer by teaching him what is happening and is likely to happen, and how he can recognise and resist the work of the devil and all his hirelings, and win through. One of the most exciting things a minister can see happen is immature Christians growing and standing on God's Word and exercising continuous, victorious authority over the powers of darkness, perhaps for the first time in their lives, and praising God from their hearts.

7.2   WHAT THE AFFLICTED CAN DO TO HELP

In a word - NOTHING - UNLESS YOU TEACH THEM WHAT THEY CAN DO! One thing is absolutely certain - those receiving ministry are going to need teaching. Teaching from the Word of God - SOLID, REPETITIVE teaching until it PENETRATES all the confusion and rebellion etc. surrounding the human spirit, and the RESTORATIVE life of Christ begins to manifest itself through each and every precious child of God. This is one of the great blessings of continuous ministry, as against the infrequent but spectacular end-of-meeting type of ministry. A once-in-a-blue-moon kind of approach affords little opportunity for the teaching essential for growth and continuous victory, and without such teaching the personal RESTORATION which the Lord desires for EVERY child of God today remains virtually unattainable. You will need to teach them how to keep the deliverance they have already fought for and won, and how vital it is to walk in the light of the New Covenant (or Testament); the need to "put to death the desires of the flesh" and all its old habits and life-styles, and learn to walk in the Spirit (Gal. 5:24-25).

They will need reassurance and encouragement and to learn to TRUST the shepherds put over them by the Great Shepherd of the Sheep (obedience is better than sacrifice!). This will be very difficult for some who have never learned to follow directions. You will need to teach them how to pray, how to resist the devil and use the right spiritual weapons and battle tactics, when to open their mouths and witness, and when to be silent and discreet because what they say may concern the confidentiality and privacy of another brother or sister in the Lord.

Assuming that the sufferer clearly needs further sessions of deliverance, the obvious question is "How often?". Many people will be of the opinion that one short prayer of faith will clean up all their hassles and, although you may suggest otherwise, you won't see them again - not for deliverance anyway. Others will want to come to EVERY deliverance group you have because they know they are *loaded* and are hungrily reaching out for everything God has for them. Don't curb or discourage them, UNLESS a shortage of counsellors or space means that someone else is missing out. Perhaps the way forward for a *normal* church programme is to hold one or two deliverance groups a week; (say) one for people available during the daytime and one after or outside of business hours for those with work-day commitments. You can then suggest that anyone sensing pressure in their soul or mind attend for deliverance as required, perhaps letting you know before she/he arrives wherever possible so you have time to refer to the personal particulars sheet on their problems, if you are using that kind of recording system to begin. This pattern works well because effective deliverance will defuse them for a while, but as the days go by, the remaining powers of darkness will re-organise themselves for a counter-attack, throwing fresh troops into the front-line. As they appear, with the subject manifesting the works of the flesh again, further deliverance should be sought for continual defusing until the war of attrition has been completely won. The subjects can help themselves and you by recognizing when they are under attack and carrying out your teaching consistently, as well as attending the next available deliverance session.

Verlie and I have noticed that, both over the long and short term, the people who make the speediest and more spectacular progress are those who:

(a) **Co-operate with and trust the ministers** MORE than their own personal understanding. This is explained in tapes and our book **"End-Time Deliverance[1]"**, but what it boils down to is they are prepared to admit that the ministers might know a little more about the subject than they do. One reason why we do not like to talk about the discernment we are given is that often IT IS NOT RECEIVED when we do!

One man told me about how his parents, whom he resented, were supposed to have made him have an operation to his brain which had changed him from a genius to a disadvantaged person. He added he had been **a child prodigy concert pianist** at the age of

---

[1] This is now entitled "End-Time Deliverance and the Holy Spirit Revival".

four years and a **black belt karate expert** at the age of three and a half years.

When I was obliged to gently ask him to trust me and to view all those events as non-events inspired by fantasy, the tears streamed down his face. He wanted to believe and trust me but the deception was too strong and he dropped out.

"But," you say, "It is dangerous to trust anyone like that!" Well, we can offer two points for consideration.

(i)   Look at the "track record" of the ministry. Is it glorifying to the Lord or is it strewn with disasters?

(ii) There is always a risk in trusting anyone, but in view of your need, it is MORE dangerous not to trust.

      The "trusties" are the Lord's best advertisement, and ours too.

(b) **Check the literature notes available week by week** and check out any new messages with the Word of God. We recommend that you work through ONE message sheet at least, per week.

(c) **Borrow or buy ONE MESSAGE cassette tape a week**, especially if, during the meetings you:

(i)   are fully under the Power of God.
(ii) receive solid ministry during the preaching.
(iii) miss the MEANING of the message for any reason at all.

(d) **Start praying for OTHERS** in your Fellowship - at

least in general terms of their welfare. The change of emphasis from self to others is a significant step forward, which is within the grasp of almost any Christian.

(e) **Attend two Christian meetings, per week**, if available, one of which is the main Sunday afternoon Deliverance and Restoration meeting. Obviously the more you fellowship with people in Restoration the more encouraged, strengthened and certain you become in your Vision of what God wants for you.

7.3 TEACHING

(i) THE WORD

"For, 'every one who calls upon the name of the Lord will be saved'. But how are men to call upon him in whom they have not believed? And how are they to believe in him of whom they have never heard? And how are they to hear without a preacher? And how can men preach unless they are sent? As it is written, 'How beautiful are the feet of those who preach good news!' But they have not all heeded the gospel; for Isaiah says, 'Lord, who has believed what he has heard from us?' *SO FAITH COMES FROM HEARING AND WHAT IS HEARD COMES THROUGH A WORD OF CHRIST."* (Romans 10:13-17).

There we have it. A word of Christ builds faith, and without faith it is impossible to please God (Heb. 11:6). The Word is also the sword of the Spirit and it is essential that the Word be read and/or heard and APPLIED regularly if they are to progress (James 1:22-25). The Christian needs to discover his or her LEGAL POSITION before God. That is to say, EVERY Christian needs to know the details of the full salvation which God has provided for us in the New Covenant through the sacrifice of His Son Jesus Christ on the Cross, and we need to know ALL that is provided for us for the winning of the spiritual warfare in which we find ourselves. In short, we need to know His promises.

When we discover the **legal, positional truth** that the Word of God declares to us, THEN we can plead our cause before the Throne, THEN we can put God in remembrance of His Word (Isa. 43:26) and ask for the spiritual power from the Throne which will bring the necessary changes in our lives so that our physical experience CONFORMS to the legal positional truth of the Word of God. For example, the Word of God commands us to **heal the sick, cast out demons, raise the dead** etc. (Matt. 10:1), and when we DO this in obedience (Matt. 28:20), our experience rises to and can conform to the Word.

Many Christians do not understand the relationship between the LEGAL position resulting from the victory of the Cross over all the hosts of darkness and the EXPERIEN-TIAL fulfilment of that victory in our lives. They rest blithely in the victory of the Cross 2000 years ago - and do nothing. They say that Jesus said *it is finished!* and there is nothing more for them to do but rest in that victory. They ignore the fact that AFTER those words the Lord later (i) RAISED Himself from the dead, (ii) ASCENDED into Heaven and (iii) was ENTHRONED at the right hand of the Father. From His Throne He then (iv) *POURED OUT THE HOLY SPIRIT* at Pentecost, and continues to exercise His sovereign will through His Spirit today.

Clearly to apply the words "It is finished!" as if they were the END of the saving process is to misunderstand the plan of salvation. Surely they mean that His earthly walk, ministry and mission in this wicked world is finished and the sacrificial price for the salvation of the spirits of men and women has been PAID, once and for all. It is not that there is nothing more for us to DO or RESPOND TO, but there is nothing more for us to PAY!

THERE IS PLENTY FOR THE CHRISTIAN TO DO - and sufferers can start to find out all about the responses required from us by reading, studying and applying the New Testament in their lives, especially obeying the Great Commission our Lord commanded His church (Matt. 28:18-20).

(a)   Victory Authority

People receiving deliverance ministry should have explained to them certain basic fundamentals, such as the need to receive the ministry of deliverance while under Christian pastoral authority; commitment to the King of the Kingdom of God, Jesus Christ our Lord; and be persuaded from God's Word that the Lord Jesus has defeated the powers of darkness on Calvary's tree (Col. 2:15). Having been crucified with Him (Rom. 6:6-8) and being born again as a child of God by receiving the Holy Spirit into their hearts (Rom. 5:5), they need to realise they no longer have to tolerate the powers of darkness hindering their desire to lead Godly lives – at least not from *within* their minds, bodies, or souls.

The Word of God says we Christian disciples have AUTHORITY[1] over ALL the POWER of the enemy. Believe it! Use it - as necessary, in Jesus' Name!

We say more about this in chapter 9.3 (i) and (iii).

---

[1] See Book 1 **"Make Yourselves Ready"** 3.1 and 3.5, also Book 2 **"Engaging the Enemy"** 5.3, 5.7 (ii) and 6.1 (iii) (b) 3, **"Christian Authority and Power"**.

14

(b)   In Christ

It is very important for sufferers to know where they stand, right now. As committed Christians, *they are "in Christ", their lives have been hidden with Christ in God* (Col. 3:3) *and His righteousness is reckoned as theirs* (Rom. 4:22-25, 1 Cor. 1:30). He has promised that none shall pluck us out of His or the Father's hand (John 10:28-29) so that provided one stands fast in the faith of Christ (Gal. 2:20), victory is assured.

(c)   Faith

Teach them to be *single-minded* about their choice in requesting deliverance. *This is not the time for double-mindedness* (James 1:6-8). Having put their hands to the deliverance plough, they must not look back like Lot's wife, double-minded about what they want or what they are doing (Luke 9:62, cf. Gen. 19:17, 26). Encourage them to trust the Lord Jesus like they have never trusted Him before (Prov. 3:5-6), because now they are indeed clay in the great Potter's hand - Praise the Lord! They have made the right choice and no matter how sharp the battle that follows they must not waver because of opposition, especially from their emotions. Their faith, motives, sincerity and conviction will surely be tested.[1] Teach them not to doubt God but rather DOUBT their DOUBTS for they know the author of them. In the garden of Eden, Adam and Eve believed the serpent and doubted God in the most unfortunate performance in the history of mankind - even allowing for the subtlety of the serpent. Christian deliverance is our opportunity to reverse that error. They must believe God's Word and doubt their doubts!

---

[1] See next chapter

There are various levels of faith in the New Testament (Mark 9:24, John 8:31-47), but the faith which SAVES means to *put your TRUST in.* Very often people think they know better than the Lord and when they have received ministry for a few sessions and seem to be coping very well they ask *"Hey, Peter, how long do I have to keep coming to a deliverance meeting? I've got other things I want to do - can you ask the Lord to speed things up a bit so that I can get cleaned up more quickly?"*

I usually explain that the Lord knows best and is personally ministering to them the way that is best for them, besides which they may need considerably more cleaning out than they think, and nothing is MORE important than that etc. etc. If I perceive that they are unhappy with this state of affairs I often agree to pray to the Lord to speed up their ministry but add the warning that things could get very hectic for them.

Invariably they come hurrying back within two weeks complaining their heads off. "Peter, Peter, I've got aches and pains throughout my body. I can't sleep. I can't get my work done. I've got continuous diarrhoea etc. etc. - what is happening to me?" I usually manage to avoid the temptation to say "Well, you asked for it, and you got it!"

These people quickly return to their "normal" ministry, thereafter letting the Lord dictate the terms of battle. He knows our frame. He knows what we can cope with and what we cannot cope with. He is in a hurry too, but He also knows what He is doing and we would be wise to let Him do it His way and at His speed. That is not only faith but wisdom also! Amen?

(d) Victory Promises and Assurances from God's Word

These are to be learnt by heart and applied with faith and

determination whenever the enemy is affecting their emotions or producing bodily symptoms, or any pressure or test of any kind. Victory must be TAKEN by the Christian!

1. **"No temptation/testing has overtaken you except what is common to a human, but God is faithful, who will not allow you to be tempted/tested beyond what you are able (to bear) but will make with the temptation/testing also the way out so that you may be able to endure (it)."** *(1 Cor. 10:13).*

This is a marvellous promise because it tells us that satan IS NOT ALLOWED to test us BEYOND what we can bear. Obviously a test must stretch our faith to its limits otherwise satan is wasting his time testing us at all, but he cannot test us BEYOND our level of faith.

For example if my level of faith measures say, 55, on an imaginary scale, it is useless satan testing me at the level of 25, 35 or even 45. He has to test me at my faith level of 55 or very close to it to have any chance of overthrowing me. This wonderful promise tells me that I can ALWAYS cope with whatever test is thrown at me, and I know that **as my faith is stretched** to overcome the challenge I become STRONGER than ever, Praise the Lord.

Sometimes sufferers receiving deliverance tell me that they can't go on anymore - it is too hard! It is usually the unclean spirit saying this, and there are at least two ways the minister can handle it.

(i) He can tell the *unclean spirit* that it does not have to suffer anymore - it has its orders to go, it is not welcome anymore, anyway.

(ii) He can remind the **sufferer** that it is NOT too hard, because the Word of God says so.

I have often said to a sufferer that if I have to choose between believing them or believing the promise of God, I'll believe God every time! And they are usually honest enough to admit that I am right - they just wanted me to know what they were going through and get some sympathy, help, encouragement, reassurance or whatever.

Here are some more wonderful promises:

2. **"Submit yourselves therefore to God. Resist the devil and he will flee from you. Draw near to God and He will draw near to you. Cleanse your hands, sinners, and purify your hearts you double-minded."** *(James 4:7-8).*

What a great Word for sufferers, especially those who are in deliverance battle and experiencing physical symptoms as they obtain releases. How do you fight spiritual warfare? Do you draw near to God or do you resist the devil? The Bible says you do BOTH! - And it also says that playing down sin in your life and deceiving yourself that you are no longer a sinner because you are a Christian (a forgiven sinner) by just "thinking positively" - as is being currently taught within the Renewal Movement - is not, repeat NOT the way to have your hearts and minds purified. This scripture tells us that submission to God is:

(i)   Resisting the devil.
(ii) Drawing near to God.
(iii) Cleansing your hands and purifying your hearts and minds from sin (i.e., everything unclean).[1]

---

[1] The relationship between sin and unclean spirits is more fully discussed in **"Your Full Salvation"** and Book (4) **"Discerning Human Nature".**

The word translated "double-minded" needs a closer look. We all know that the secular sciences of psychiatry and psychology have erred in understanding the word "psych" to mean only mind and rarely give any recognition at all to the existence of the soul or the human spirit. In their understanding, "it's all in the mind". However the Word of God makes some very clear distinctions indicating that the soul-life[1] or animal-life of man involves the huge area of the emotions and that the mind is only *part of* the soulish area.

"Double-minded" means literally "two-souled" and so the scripture commands us to purify our hearts which will have the effect of making us single-minded or single-souled for the Lord, and this involves the whole spiritual nature of a human being, not just the mind.

3.   "God ... has taken it (the Old Covenant of justice and death) out the way, nailing it to the Cross; putting off the rulers and authorities (of darkness). He (God) made them an open spectacle, triumphing over them in Him (Jesus)." *(Col. 2:14b-15).*

The Cross of Jesus is the *BASIS* of our Victory over every demon - what more is there to say? They know it - and now WE know it! Perhaps we can highlight the power contained in this verse by explaining the force of the word "spectacle". Bible scholars tell us that when the Roman military legions returned to Rome after successful conquests over the nations, they would camp outside the city until preparations for a triumphant victory parade was organised, and at a given signal the victorious army would make its grand entry. The general of the army would bring

[1] See "Spirit and Soul" in **"Your Full Salvation".**

up the rear and all the kings he had vanquished in battle would be dragged behind his chariot in rags and chains.

This is the open spectacle to which the apostle Paul alludes. The Greek word is only used once in the New Testament and the picture painted for us is that the Lord Jesus triumphed over all the demonic rulers and authorities through the Cross, dragging them in rags and chains as captives (so to speak) behind His chariot, in His triumphant procession. Truly He has led captivity captive.

Those things which held us captive in spiritual chains are now themselves the captives, through the blood of Christ. Hallelujah! No wonder the *Good News Bible* translates verse 15:

> **"And on that Cross Christ freed Himself from the power of the spiritual rulers and authorities;** *he made* **a** *public spectacle of them by leading them as captives in his victory procession."*

Anyone who *believes* the Word of God, and *knows, understands* and *applies* this verse should never lose another battle, but of course, being the frail and fleshly creatures we are[1]... As the apostle Paul says, "it is not the Word of God that fails" (Rom. 9:6).

4. **"But thanks be to God, who in Christ always leads us in triumph...."** *(2 Cor. 2:14a)*

There are SOME Christians who know what it is to walk continuously in victory and Paul is obviously referring to himself and other members of his apostolic band.

---

[1] See Chapter 9 "Failures"

WE (Christian ministers and Christian sufferers) can attain that victory walk - the Bible says so - "Christ ALWAYS leads us in triumph!"

If there was ONE phrase of scripture that I could burn indelibly into every Christian heart, spirit and mind, it would be this one. It needs no explanations but there are some who find it hard to believe. Perhaps when we understand the next victory promise it becomes easier.

5. **"And we know that to those who love God, God works all things together for good, to those called according to His purpose."**
   (Rom. 8:28).

Do you believe that God brings good out of evil for those who belong to Him and love Him? Of course you do and so must every sufferer receiving deliverance if they want to march forward in their Christian walk.

Joseph said the same thing to his brothers, the sons of Israel, after he revealed himself and was reconciled to them in Egypt. Referring to the fact that they had sold him into slavery in order to get rid of him, he said, **"You meant it for evil but God meant it for good!"** (Gen. 50:20).

God works all things - All Things - ALL THINGS for GOOD - for HIS PEOPLE. Even pagans sing "every cloud has a silver lining", and they don't have a promise from Almighty God to stand on; how much more should Christians be able to rest in the assurance of God's Word. *Blessed is the believer who, when passing through the vale of misery, uses it for a well of life-giving water* (Ps. 85:5-6).

All these verses need to be taught every oppressed person - repetitively - until they penetrate into the minds and through to the human SPIRIT so that they become part of the moment to moment consciousness of the child of God. Other well-known positive victory verses such as Romans 8:31 and Philippians 4:13 can be added to your victory teaching as well.

(ii) KEEPING THEIR DELIVERANCE AND THE COVENANT

(a) Relapses

Now relapses happen in most areas of Christian experience (such as various degrees of back-sliding) and they can easily happen in the area of deliverance if care is not taken. Even a soundly converted Christian can backslide but that will in no way deter an evangelist from trying to convert others to Christ, by the grace of God. The strange thing is that back-sliders, and other Christians experiencing barriers to growth, are not thought of in any way as problems to evangelism, in the sense that it is going to hold any evangelist back from carrying out his calling. But unfortunately in the field of healing and deliverance, should a sufferer relapse or backslide, it is often held up as some kind of mountainous problem, and the suggestion is usually that we ought to pack up immediately and permanently. Such is the weak faith and trust in God's Word by many Christians. The same truth applies to both areas of ministry - evangelism *AND* deliverance, so that having put our hand to the deliverance plough, we should proceed with all vigour and encouragement and truly trust in the knowledge that God will bring all things right in the end (Rom. 8:26-28). The problem and the answer really lie, I believe, in the human will, which is by nature besieged by double-mindedness and prone, like Adam, to listen to the voice of doubt rather than the Word of God.

We say more about this under **Lapses** in 8.1 (iii) (d)

(b) Human will

Genesis 1:26 tells us that man is made in the image of God and certainly this applies to man in the area of WILL. Man has the capacity to make Godly decisions - important and effective decisions - regardless of his FEELINGS, so that the step of repentance, for example, becomes a decision of the will rather than an emotion, although emotion MAY be present and may be very helpful in reaching a state of repentance (2 Cor. 7:9-10); but the important thing is that we can make the right choices by decisions of the will no matter what fear or doubt might try to divert us. I used to detest, for example, getting out of bed at 6.00 a.m. to go to Theological College Chapel before the day of studying began. The worship of the Lord was not the problem - it was the early rise on a cold winter's morning. When the alarm went at 6.00 a.m. it seemed that every part of my being screamed out, "Just another five minutes in bed!" The bed was so warm - and the morning so cold. But even though every part of me (my flesh) WANTED to stay in my warm bed, I was forced, like millions of workers in every country, to take the plunge and spring out, into the coldness of the room. It was a *decision of the will* which gave me victory over all my fleshly and emotional feelings and I could choose the right course in spite of all opposition. We ALL can, and do, choose the course that we must, rather than the course we would like, especially as our Christian maturity increases. However we should note that though the spirit is willing, the flesh is weak (Matt. 26:41) and that very often the flesh will unfortunately overrule the human spirit and will, UNLESS the sufferer is strongly MOTIVATED by a sense of desperation or is under conviction by the Holy Spirit (Rom. 7:18-21). Flesh, of course, is the desired and normal dwelling place of unclean spirits (v.18), which explains its weakness. We will discuss this more fully in Book 4.

(c) Causes

When we ask ourselves how demons enter into a human, very often the answer is through wrong attitudes or a non-Godly life-style; what the New Testament calls "walking according to the flesh" (2 Cor. 10:2-3 literal). If John Brown is curious about drugs or seances or mystic religions etc. he must expect to be infected. If he visits sex movies he must expect sexual spirits to move into his body and thoughts, and affect his life-style. Rebellion against parents or any authority established in the design of God, and especially against the moral law of God as revealed in the New Testament, will create a demon's picnic in the rebellious. The scriptures tell us that we are to **"abstain from fleshly lusts *which war against the soul"*** (1 Peter 2:11) and too many people have ignored this warning to their own cost.

There is an old saying that **"Birds of a feather flock together"** which means that you can tell a man's character by the company he keeps.

For example, if a young man keeps company with drunkards, he will become a drunkard, likewise with thieves, adulterers, homosexuals, drug junkies etc. A young boy once gave an excellent talk in front of his classmates against the evils and stupidity of smoking cigarettes. Later when he went to work he was surrounded by smokers, and before long he began smoking. This led to marijhuana and then hard drugs. He became unreliable and unable to cope with daily living. A failed suicide attempt followed.

Disappointing? Yes, but understandable. It is like the growth of cane. You plant it in your garden in one spot and the next thing you know it is shooting up all over the place, with runners travelling underground and colonising new growth every few feet. Kingdoms of unclean spirits are like that - seeking to colonise in every available unsuspecting soul from within the company people keep.

Christians have always been taught that they should love the sufferer, but hate the sin in the sufferer's life. If you, as Christ's minister, sympathise with the SIN as well as the sufferer you are doing more harm than good and your ability in Christ to achieve something effective will be greatly weakened. Pouring out compassion on a sufferer can be a beautiful Christian act, but if on the other hand you are supporting and "feeding" an unclean spirit of say, **self-pity,** that is counter-productive. Not only is the unclean kingdom strengthened but, transference to you is not impossible as you "sympathise".

Therefore it may be fine to sympathise with a sufferer, but not with his or her sickness or uncleanness.

The good news is that the desire of unclean spirits to transfer can clearly be controlled by Christians. Consider the case of two school teachers from the country who came to the city and were receiving deliverance. They had been involved in **spiritualism** or **spiritism** and were hearing voices which were talking inside them and telling them what to do all the time. When the ministry began to bear down on this situation the voices began to talk inside and the teachers were able to tell those who were ministering to them what they were saying, so that we knew what these things were planning. (At that stage of our ministry none of the deliverance team had been given the gift of hearing the demons arguing amongst themselves from within the sufferer). At one point they were saying, "Oh, the pattern's breaking up, the pattern's breaking up, what'll we do, what'll we do?" As they panicked, one spirit suggested inside, "Oh, I know, we'll go to B...", (B... being a close friend of theirs who also had plenty of hang-ups as well - it wouldn't have been any trouble for them to move into B...). So they said, "Ha, ha, we're going to B... we're going to B...". So the ministers put B... out of bounds in the Name of Jesus and then they said, "Oh, we can't go there, we can't go there, we can't go to B... . What'll we do, what'll we do? The pattern's breaking, the pattern's breaking up." And it was too, praise God. That gives you some idea of the rapport that one can have with the subject who can advise what is happening inside them, or when the minister can hear with spiritual ears what the demons are saying to each other. The demons planned to transfer into B..., but due to our knowledge of our authority to bind and to loose in Jesus' Name, we were able to foil their plans for transfer. Transferences can take place during perfectly honourable occupations and activities, as we have seen when discussing the dangers of counselling or ministering in Book 2, chapter 5.5 under the heading of "Transference of spirits."

However, the main sources of demonisation are, of course: (i) by means of the *HEREDITARY DEPOSIT* in the human soul transferred from the souls of the natural father and mother through conception (Rom. 5:12)[1] and (ii) *ENVIRON-MENTAL*[2] *SOURCES* during growing up. Any close contact, especially becoming "one flesh" through sexual intercourse, invites transferences from soul to soul, and this soul-link no doubt explains why many husbands and wives grow to think alike over the years.

---

[1] For a full explanation, see Book 4 **"Discerning Human Nature"** or more briefly in **"The Re-incarnation Deception"** and **"End-Time Deliverance"**.
[2] Here we mean family support, training and culture.

(d) Application

It becomes necessary, after deliverance has been effected and the demons despatched, to ATTEND TO THE PRIOR ATTITUDES, THE WEAKNESSES which have allowed them access in the first place. We who are Christians are supposed to have the mind of Christ (1 Cor. 2:16) and to be transformed by the renewal of our minds (Rom. 12:2). We must put on the helmet of salvation (Eph. 6:17) to protect our minds against the (spiritual) rulers and authorities (Eph. 6:12) and thus develop a new thought "style" that we might be conformed to the image of God's Son (Rom. 8:29) and no longer subject to the elemental spirits of the universe (Gal. 4:9).

All this will require decisions of the will as a matter of SELF-discipline and your people will need the help of God's Spirit, exercised through PASTORAL discipline and fellowship with other Christians in the body of Christ, in obedience to the New Covenant. They must put the desires of the flesh to death by the exercise of their enlightened hearts and wills - say "NO!" to old patterns of behaviour, and walk in the Spirit (Gal. 5:24-25). AFTER THE DEMONS ARE OUT, THE ORIGINAL ATTITUDES AND WILL OF SUFFERERS MUST CHANGE AND THEIR LIVES BE REBUILT AS FITTING IN THE LORD FOR NEW CREATURES, EXCHANGING OLD HABITS FOR NEW!

If they can't do this, then we have all wasted our time. Another batch of rulers and authorities that are always present or nearby are going to say, "Now, there is a nice rebellious type; just what we have been looking for." And the sufferer is back where they started, if not worse than before! That is no good to them and that is no good to you who minister.

(e)   Attitude

The RESPONSE of the sufferer can be very important in relation to the progress that a ministry is making, whether deliverance or healing or both. I can think of ten (10) areas requiring a positive response of faith:

1.   The *sincerity* of the sufferer in desiring the ministry, and the ability to stand firm in the Word of God regardless of all discouragement by well-meaning Pastors and Christians, or false brethren, who have not caught the vision, etc. (Eph. 6:10-14, James 5:7-11, Phil. 3:2,17-4:1).

   Also, the sufferer's ability to:-

2.   *Catch the revelation of God* about sin and demons, and the extent of our infection, i.e. to understand something of the PROBLEM. (Eph. 2:2, 6:12, Matt. 12:38-45).

3.   *KNOW when they are manifesting* uncleanness (Matt. 15:18- 20), and immediately-

4.   *Bring their spiritual, Christian weapons into operation* when they are under spiritual attack (i.e., manifesting). For example, Praise, Prayer, Authority, Word, etc. Their cassette players should be worn out by PRAISE tapes! (1 Cor. 12:4-11, Eph. 6:14-18, James 4:7-8, Phil. 4:4-9).

5.   *Cope with manifestations and actual deliverance day by day* in the context of their ongoing daily responsibilities in the home and at work. (Rom. 8:31-39, Phil. 1:27-30, 3:12-17, 4:13).

6.   *Follow the counselling* given, putting away and over-ruling all rebellious inclinations (Heb. 13:7,17; Phil. 2:12-13), knowing that their source within them is unclean (Eph. 2:2). Such counsel, of course, should only be that which is necessary for effective deliverance ministry, and provided the sufferer can see the need for whatever is counselled the minister can usually obtain their co-operation.

7.   *Trust those who are ministering BEYOND the counselling given, even more than THEIR OWN ideas,* to the point of discarding personal (deceptive) notions when required (Prov. 3:5, John 10:4,5,14 cf. 2 Cor. 8:5).

As we wrote in 7.2 (a) this sounds dangerous, but quite obviously sufferers are only going to put their souls in the hands of a Christian deliverance minister of whom they have heard at least some good reports. When they arrive at the meetings they may be tuned in spiritually for evidence of the presence of the risen Christ in the meeting and in the ministers. They don't have to stay, but if they do, wanting your help in Christ, then it is very often necessary for them to put down their preconceived ideas (usually polluted) and trust that the Holy Spirit will guide you on their behalf (See Book 1, Chap. 4).

People who come to you because they are desperate and have nothing to lose except their problems will probably trust you immediately and make speedy progress. Others less desperate may find it difficult to trust you, and barriers will need to be overcome before they can really advance into full Restoration.

8.   *Keep looking ahead to* the ultimate victory, and not looking back until it is achieved, i.e., the personal

determination TO WIN in the Name of the Lord Jesus (Luke 9:62, Gal. 6:9, Phil. 3:12-4:1, Rev. 2:1-3:22).

9. *REJOICE in the SOLUTION* provided by Jesus Christ our Lord, that is, the provision of a FULL SALVATION within the vision of the End Time and the RESTORA-TION of the whole true Church; and rejoice in belong-ing! (Phil. 4:4-7, 1 Thess. 5:16-18, 1 Peter 1:5-9, James 1:2-4).

10. *Keep the Word of God* in the New Covenant and *walk in the Spirit,* more and more, moment to moment (John 3:36, Gal. 5:16-25, Eph. 5:15-20, Phil. 1:27-2:2).

Sometimes a sufferer's attitude may appear fine on the surface but progress is slow. This may be due to a hidden and unconscious resistance to the ministry. This problem is discussed in the next chapter under the sub-heading "Letting Go!"

(f)   The New Covenant

Obviously the New Testament (or Covenant), i.e. the new agreement God has established for mankind is our stand-ard of truth, authority and the revealed guidance of God for His children, and it carries both *blessings AND responsi-bilities.* Your people will need to be taught that the Bible is a record of two covenants or testaments - the Old Testa-ment which operated until the Lord Jesus Christ ratified for believers the New Covenant or Testament with His own precious blood, shed on the Cross. In other words, Christ has obtained a new deal for people seeking God and they can find out all about it by reading the New Testament of the Bible.

Some Christians try to continue to live under the Old

Covenant, insisting on keeping some or all of its religious laws - what Jesus called putting new wine into old wineskins. However a moments thought will reveal the foolishness of this.

If you had a fine home, but it was heavily mortgaged and one day your bank manager rang you and offered you a new deal with a much better financial arrangement for you, would you appreciate the new deal or would you insist on continuing with the harsher conditions pertaining to the first mortgage contract?

Hebrews chapter 8 tells us that the New Covenant is a much better deal than the Old Covenant, for the people of God.

In brief, this new deal is like a narrow path up the side of a mountain. There are all sorts of side-tracks leading off the narrow path which God has marked "DANGER!". While we keep to God's path of the New Covenant for our lives, we can safely negotiate our way through this wicked world, into the heavens.

However, satan has marked all the dangerous side-tracks with HIS signposts such as "*Permissive Pleasure*", "*Occult Truth*", "*Power through Politics*", "*Gods of Eastern Mysticism*", "*Healing through Hypnosis*", "*Sexual Liberty*" and "*Do your own Thing*" etc. etc. but which in fact lead to slavery, darkness and destruction (2 Peter 2:18-19). So the restrictions of the New Testament upon our lives are for our own good - our safety. By trust and obedience we can negotiate this life in peace and security in spite of the beggarly and elemental spirits of the universe. To stray into the side-tracks, however, brings us into disobedience against God *and out from under Jesus' protection,* exposing us to the fiery attacks of evil. Our footing gives way and we tumble down into blackness but, praise God, Jesus remains our way of escape or rescue (deliverance) for all those who call upon Him to deliver them at any stage of our journey through life (Matt. 14:30-31, Acts 2:21). As you know, the New Covenant requires showing forth the fruit of the Spirit in our lives; obedience and submission to the Lord, prayer and praise, fellowship in the Body of Christ - to name just a few necessities. It is as Jesus said: *"If you CONTINUE in my WORD, you are TRULY my disciples, and you will know the TRUTH and the truth will make you FREE" (John 8:31-33).*

So the Christian who is being delivered must proceed to walk more and more in the Holy Spirit day by day. The alternative is to be exposed to the danger of a relapse and a last state possibly seven times worse than the first! (Matt. 12:43-45).

In a phrase, the person being delivered is to *"be FAITHFUL to the calling with which you have been called" (2 Thess. 1:11, 2 Tim. 1:8-9, Phil. 3:14).*

(iii) PRAYER WEAPONS

Teach sufferers to pray in a way that will speed the day of their new freedom in Christ. When they were first converted, they may have prayed something like this:

> *"Dear Lord Jesus,*
>
> *I am a sinner and I acknowledge my unworthiness before you. I repent and turn from my sins and ask you to forgive me, and cleanse me by your precious Blood. I want you to be my Lord and my God all the days of my life.*

*And I ask you to now fill me with your Holy
Spirit and lead me in your ways.*

Thank you, Lord Jesus."

Although this may be considered an elementary conversion or sinners prayer, it nevertheless contains a *powerful
basis for DAILY prayers,* even for mature Christians, viz:-

(a)   FORGIVENESS OF SINS

Did not our Lord teach us to pray daily for the forgiveness
of our sins? The Lord's Prayer is clearly a daily prayer *("give
us this day")* and yet its strongest human emphasis is on
the need for forgiveness. We say this because the section
on forgiveness is the only part expanded on by the Lord
when He taught the prayer (Matt. 6:9-15). The Bible says
sin is lawlessness (1 John 3:4) and that failure to confess
sins may be a barrier to healing (James 5:16), so I encourage us all to engage in at least a daily cleansing prayer to
the Lord, if not even more often, as necessary. We cleanse
our outer skin by washing our face, hands and teeth daily
and feel better for having done so; how much better, then,
will we feel when we know daily cleansing of our inward
parts - in our minds, souls, emotions and spirits? Keep
short accounts with the Lord.

This is not to be arbitrarily legalistic but it is important not
to fall into the trap of believing that because we Christians
are "in Christ" that we have daily forgiveness *automatically*
without asking for it. There is a sense in which we do enjoy
continuous forgiveness because we belong to the Lord but
we should never presume on God's grace by failing to
repent daily. Far from being a negative and legalistic exercise, it is a most liberating one as our spirit experiences

the peace of God which passes all understanding through fresh reconciliation and un-blocked union with our gracious Lord.

(b) CONTINUOUS DELIVERANCE

Do you want to speed up your complete deliverance from unclean spirits? Then make your petition to the Lord along the lines of the Lord's Prayer - "but deliver us from evil" (or "the evil one"). *Let Him know what you want* in this regard, that He may hear your prayer and answer you gladly; but spell it out to the Lord plainly - ask and you shall receive - and He will delight to answer you as quickly as is good for you.

(c) THE PROTECTION OF THE BLOOD

As he went to do battle with **Goliath, David** was offered King Saul's armour, but it was useless because it didn't fit. He was then clothed in God's spiritual armour - that "fitted" perfectly. The Lord's armour fits perfectly over His obedient children who daily walk with Him (1 Sam. 17:34-39).

The basic principle of the Lord God Almighty who keeps His people SAFE (Psalm 121) lies at the very heart of our salvation. It is the message of the Bible. We are saved (kept safe) from the Destroyer and all his wiles and works, that is, their consequences, when we KNOW how to protect ourselves with spiritual weapons (see Appendix M).

This prayer principle can also be drawn from the Lord's Prayer - *"and lead us not into temptation"* - which is usually translated today - *"do not put us to the test"*. We ask the Lord to spare us testing which is another way of saying: "Protect us, Lord, from all the attacks (wiles and works) of the enemy". Thus we come to an important principle to be added to the conversion prayer - preservation or protection! In the Old Covenant **the blood of the Passover Lamb** prevented the destroyer from destroying the children of Israel (Exod. 12:23) and the New Covenant tells us that **Jesus is OUR Passover Lamb sacrificed for us** (1 Cor. 5:7) and that **faith in His Blood** (Rom. 3:25 KJV) **becomes a shield of faith** with which to quench all the fiery darts of the evil one (Eph. 6:16).

Therefore, when sufferers pray, they should ask the Lord Jesus - at least DAILY - to cover them, and their **believing** household if they are responsible for one, with His precious Blood, the Blood of the true Passover Lamb, for His Blood has ratified a New Covenant wherein He covenants, amongst many other promises, to (I) deliver them from evil, (II) that none shall pluck them out of His hand, (III) to destroy the works of the devil and (IV) that they shall be GUARDED BY THE POWER OF GOD through faith (1 Peter 1:5). It is not blood guarding them because of some kind of magical formula; it is the Blood of the *Covenant,* with all the promises which have been ratified with the Blood (Heb. 9:18). They should pray then - each day - that the Blood of the Covenant cover them and the CHRIS-TIAN[1] members of their family from all the fiery darts of the evil one, and that they be kept safe by the power of God. (See also Appendix M)

(d) THE FULNESS OF THE (HOLY) SPIRIT

Of course, they will need to pray to *be filled with the Holy Spirit* (Eph. 5:18) because we conquer **"not by might (of an**

---

[1] Sad to say, the Blood of Jesus ought NOT to be prayed upon anyone about whom there is any doubt that their salvation or redemption has been redeemed with Christ's Blood. This may be equivalent to "profaning the Blood" (1 Cor. 11:27) and is highly dangerous.

army) **nor by power** *(of man)* **but by My Spirit" says the Lord of hosts** *(Zech. 4:6).* It is not sufficient to be filled with the Spirit last year - or even last week; the literal meaning of the apostle's command is "CONTINUE to be filled" and each day as a Christian will bring its fresh challenges which they will not be able to meet in their own strength. *"Walking in the Spirit"* is, of course, not simply a day by day exercise but ideally a moment to moment experience. They should pray each day to be filled with the Holy Spirit, as the Lord has commanded, knowing that He is pleased to answer prayers that are in accordance with His expressed will for us. **There is not much point in getting rid of UNCLEAN spirits unless they are replaced in the soul by the HOLY Spirit,** that Christians might be truly filled with all the fulness of Christ and of God! This fulness gives Christians the enabling POWER to do what the Lord wants done!

It will also mean that they will not find it difficult to acknowledge Jesus as *"my Lord and my God"* (John 20:28, 1 Cor. 12:3). They will have already renounced the devil and all his works when they began deliverance, so now they need to fix their spiritual eyes (the *"eyes of your hearts"* - Eph. 1:18) on Jesus and in conscious submission to His Lordship they will find peace and true freedom (Isa. 26:3).

(e) PROSPERITY

As satan is the god of this world and exercises his worldly pressures through world finances, many Christians will find themselves beset by a spirit of poverty which flows from the curse of witchcraft (Deut. 28). As this, and all such curses, are legally broken by Christ, it is good for us to break free from this bondage and appropriate the blessing of prosperity in God, both SPIRITUAL AND MATERIAL, PROVIDED we ask for *the wisdom of Christ* to guide us in the use of the

Lord's provision. This subject is a book in itself[1] but suffice to say here that the blessing of material prosperity is a good thing for the people of God to ask of the Lord; again emphasizing, *provided our motives* are pleasing to Him.

Summary

Thus we have suggested that sufferers being delivered from the shackles of satan could be taught to pray daily for a five-fold blessing, as under:

1. Forgiveness of sins.
2. Deliverance from the evil one.
3. The Covering Protection of the Blood of the Lamb.
4. The Fulness of the Spirit.
5. Prosperity and Wisdom.

and DON'T FORGET TO TELL HIM YOU LOVE HIM! The private worship and praise of the Lord should not be neglected.

(f)   OTHER PRAYER WEAPONS

1.   Pray in the Spirit

If the Lord has given the sufferer an (unknown) tongue with which to pray to Him and praise Him, this should be encouraged as a daily exercise also. Too many Christians have the gift of a tongue and do not use it at all or only rarely. When we pray in a tongue, our spirit prays PERFECT prayers because the words are **supplied** by the Holy Spirit, even though they are **spoken** *by* the human spirit (1 Cor. 14:14). How foolish we are, then, to neglect this gracious gift of communion

---

[1] Discussed more fully in **"Your Full Salvation"**

with the Lord - spirit to Spirit. So it is good to remind sufferers - indeed any Christian - to pray always with (by/in)[1] the spirit (Eph. 6:18, Jude 20).

2. Your Confession of Faith

The Word of God says that the saints overcome the enemy *"by the Blood of the Lamb and the Word of their testimony"* (Rev. 12:11). See Appendix K for a **Confession of Faith**, the framework for which was originally drawn up by **John Osteen**, but now slightly revised for our purposes.

This Confession is a statement, a testimony of our LEGAL position in Christ because of the victory of His shed Blood, and therefore fulfils exactly the scriptural requirements for overcoming the enemy. Stating or testifying to our LEGAL rights, by faith, daily, audibly, brings to us the victories we have believed for, and declared by faith.

3. Prayer and Fasting

There are plenty of good books on Christian Fasting available. I found **Rev. Franklyn Hall's** materials (**"Fasting Faith Books"**) very helpful as well as **"God's Chosen Fast"** by **Arthur Wallis**. Whereas I have found it necessary to occasionally fast for one or two weeks (the longer it goes the easier it gets), the good Lord has convicted me to fast two days a week (yes, like the Pharisee - Luke 18:10-12). Such regular short fasts are probably the hardest in terms of food control, but they provide a much-needed regular

---

[1] The Greek preposition used here can be translated "in," "with" or "by" i.e. "by means of".

discipline in my life over the lusts of the flesh (1 Cor. 9:27, Gal. 5:24).

When praying, don't forget your **Heart's Desires** (Ps. 37:4).

4.   Exercise

You may ask why exercise is listed under prayer weapons. It is obviously not a **prayer** weapon but it can give opportunity for prayer, especially as the sun rises on your local golf links. Surrounded by ducks and ducklings, rabbits and kangaroos, trees and brooks, one can find prayer comes easily in the midst of the wonder of God's creation.

Not everyone can find work in these days of advanced technology, and even those who have jobs don't always get sufficient **physical** activity to exercise their bodies. However most of us can get some form of exercise to keep our lungs, heart and limbs functioning, enough to burn off the food we eat.

It is very important to strike the right balance of food (energy) supply and work (energy) expended. Our bodies are TEMPLES of God's Holy Spirit, and without these temples we could not pray, they are the MEANS of our prayer weapons. They belong to God and are for honouring God (1 Cor. 6:19-20 cf. 9:24-27), so let's look after them.

5.   Renunciation Prayers

These can be directed to the Lord (in respectful terms) or to the unclean spirits (with authority). The **Curse**

Breaking prayer¹ comes under this heading, as does a renouncing of **Ancestral** (generational) pollution, and all unclean attacks upon your spirit, soul and body.²

Don't get excited and get it mixed up and wrong. You blast the ENEMY, not the Lord! You renounce the ENEMY, not the Lord! When you have finished telling the enemy what you think of him and where to go (with his fiery darts - Eph. 6:16), then praise and thank the Lord for giving us (His disciples) *authority over ALL the POWER of the enemy (Luke 10:19).*

This section on prayer may seem to have a very self-centred "gi'me! gi'me! gi'me!" theme but what I mean to emphasise is that the Lord has taught us to ask for daily essentials, especially spiritual blessings. However, let us remember to teach sufferers and other growing Christians to always surround their petitions with praise and thanksgiving from their hearts and remember to uphold others in prayer who are in need also. **When sufferers begin to intercede for OTHERS in prayer, it is clear their soulish selfishness is being healed** because the measure of our SELFISHNESS IS AN IMPORTANT MEASURE OF OUR DEMONISATION.

And don't forget to tell Him YOU LOVE HIM!

Even though the hearts of your sufferers may seem cold and uninterested in prayer communication with the Father they should not be deceived by emotions or lack of them. Love is not just feelings alone, which change from moment to moment, but love expresses RELATIONSHIP, CONTINUOUS

¹ See Book 1 **"Make Yourselves Ready"** Appendix E.
² See Appendix L.

RELATIONSHIP, especially between a Father and His sons and daughters.

The relationship stands, regardless of feelings or emotional conflict, so that if a sufferer IS a child of God, he (or she) can truly say, "I love you, Father!" Such an expression of faith and relationship will *break the coldness,* so that the emotion of affection will flow and grow immeasureably.

To love and be loved in return is one of the great reasons for, and blessings of, our existence. To know love for our Heavenly Father, because He first loved us (1 John 4:19) through our Lord Jesus Christ, is the greatest blessing of all - and it is ours because we belong to Christ. (Rom. 5:5, 8:9)

PRAISE THE LORD!

(iv) FELLOWSHIP

(a) Worship and Praise

Regular fellowship with Christians, especially for the purpose of worship, praise and thanksgiving, is utterly essential, unless you want a long drawn-out deliverance. As they minister to the Lord, *He inhabits the praises of His people* (Psalm 22:3). This is basic, fundamental Christianity and must not be overlooked.

Just to give you a few examples of how praise and thanksgiving are used as weapons of spiritual warfare, we note the following:-

   (i)   Trumpets and a great shout (probably of praise to the name of YAHWEH) brought down the walls of **Jericho** (Josh. 6:16-20). Shouting is a normal expression of Hebrew worship (2 Chron. 20:19, Ps. 47:1, Isa. 12:6, 42:11, Jer. 31:7, Zech. 9:9) but if you did that in many historic church buildings today, even at an appropriate place in the worship, and with a good spirit, the wardens would probably escort you to the exit.

(ii) The advance guard or spearhead of the Hebrew army going into battle was not the cavalry nor the infantry nor the armoured divisions, so to speak, but - wait for it - the singers and musicians (2 Chron. 20:19-22). What brave men - and what FAITH in their God! I understand this tradition was followed by Scottish Highland Regiments during World War II, but WHAT they played on their bag-pipes was composed by their bards or minstrels, and may not always have been the praise of God.

(iii) The playing of a minstrel brought the power of God upon **Elisha** (2 Kings 3:15).

(iv) **David's** psalm-playing music caused an unclean spirit to depart (lit. "turn aside") from **King Saul** (1 Sam. 16:14-23).

We do not say much on this subject only because it is a principle EVERY Christian should know and practice, and there are plenty of good books available covering it.

(b) Sharing

Christians gather together also to **(i) bear one anothers' burdens** (Gal. 6:2) (ii) **confess sins to one another** (iii) **pray for each other** (James 5:16) (iv) **care for one**

another (v) **suffer** and **rejoice together** (1 Cor. 12:25-26), and (vi) **comfort one another** with the Word of Christ's return for His people (1 Thess. 4:18). Sharing in the way that the Word of God encourages us is a wonderful privilege, but *LET US BE CAREFUL WHAT WE SHARE!* Let us make a clear distinction right now between general encouragement that comes from sharing, and counselling for the deliverance ministry. You do not want people who are receiving deliverance ministry turning to every Tom, Dick and Harry for counsel (gossip?) and this is a rule on which you should insist. It is far better for them not to talk at all (let alone continuously) about their problems needing deliverance EXCEPT WITH A DELIVERANCE COUNSELLOR. They should learn to fix their minds on the Lord Jesus Christ and victory and talk about those things. When they read the Bible, they should not neglect passages which relate to all the other unsearchable riches of Christ (non-deliverance!). By all means they may discuss with their fellow sufferers all the positive, victorious aspects of Christianity, but they should remember that *they need ministry too;* they are also going through transitory stages and are perhaps unable to give *unclouded* counsel. Many of them will not have the capacity to cope with their OWN problems, let alone another's list of problems dumped on them. Therefore sufferers should be discreet, selective, and NOT GOSSIP about themselves or others, which can be an unclean compulsive problem for some. Teach them to distinguish between *gossip,* and *witnessing* which glorifies Jesus.

Sufferers should **encourage, comfort, uphold** and **pray** for one another but leave the specific counselling to the counsellors! If someone asks them for advice and the questions lie in the area of deliverance, such questions should be referred on to a recognised counsellor immediately, without getting involved. Wherever the gifts of the Spirit are manifested, satan attempts to move in quickly with his coun-terfeit gifts and we are not unaware of his designs. Obedi-ence brings blessing and disobedience brings trouble, so these rules should be observed consistently. Rebellious people can be reminded that such rules are drawn from the New Testament.

(c) Conduct

Remember that the conditions of sufferers probably have some outward manifestations in the form of bad habits, and as deliverance takes place, you will need to teach them to do their utmost to break habits which bind them. If their problems consist of lust, smoking, swearing and drink-ing, it is obviously unhelpful if they are going to watch sex movies, chain-smoke, give vent to their tongues and keep company with their old drinking mates. As we have said before, every effort must be made to control the "flesh" and its desires by decisions of the will which are in conformity with their new life in Christ.

Some failures should not cause too much despair PRO-VIDED (i) they are endeavouring sincerely to keep the New Covenant, (ii) REPENT and (iii) re-apply themselves to the challenge. Repeated failure should be referred to the Pastor or Deliverance Minister for further counselling and correction.

(d) Visiting other fellowships

People receiving deliverance from you should *not* attend Christian meetings other than those at their own home church, without checking with their deliverance minister. This may be something of a surprise but a moment's reflection will help you to see the need and the value of this. Some meetings, especially those where there is a welling of praise to God, may easily stir a battle within sensitive sufferers or those who manifest dramatically. On rare occasions the more blessed and anointed the meeting the better it may be for SOME sufferers to stay away, **UNLESS you can be sure there are experienced Pastors on hand to minister deliverance, if necessary.**

A greatly blessed meeting may cause SOME sufferers to become disruptive and the worship may be thrown into disarray, not to mention the destructive public spectacle that satan likes to create. On the other hand, with the presence of experienced ministers, a seeming "disaster" can be God's opportunity to show forth His Power and the worship can really "take off" in the Spirit during such incidents, as the assembly supports the ministers in deliverance battle. However, the sufferer's deliverance ministers are entitled to know, and should know, of the worship practices of sufferers so that they can be counselled accordingly, for their own good! *In the vast majority of cases no restrictions are necessary.*

In *unusual* cases it may be necessary to advise sufferers to stay away from any other form of (corporate) spiritual activity, except in the company of trained ministers, until deliverance is well advanced. When situations like this arise because of heavy demonisation, the sufferer is normally quite happy to co-operate because "they" hate going to alive Christian fellowships anyway.

Unfortunately, at the time of writing, there are not too many meetings where trained and experienced deliverance ministers are available, and consequently this seems the only responsible policy to adopt on behalf of sufferers who are looking to you for guidance under Christ. Deliverance ministers may not be legally responsible before the courts of the world, but they are certainly morally responsible to God for each soul entrusted to (and under) their care. Acts of disobedience or non-compliance etc., by sufferers absolves the ministers of this responsibility, of course.

(e) Discretion

Remember that receiving deliverance is a delicate matter for many people and, while its necessary humility is a blessing, discretion by ministers and sufferers alike regarding *names* and *cases* known to them, is an important discipline of the Bible, in that God's people are not to gossip (Rom. 1:29) and should be "slow to speak" (James 1:19). Better still, keep silent ABOUT OTHERS unless you have the permission of the appropriate person to speak of their circumstances. If sufferers can follow the directions and counselling, it will not be long before they themselves can testify to the whole world of what the Lord Jesus Christ has done for THEM. *Gossip is unclean; genuine testimony is Holy!* HALLELUJAH!

CHAPTER 8

OPPOSITION

8.1 OPPOSITION TO THE SUFFERER

The previous chapter dealt generally with what the sufferer can expect after deliverance commences, but we now need to add some more specific comments to what has already been written. For this purpose we have divided our comments into three sections as follows:

(i) OPPOSITION WITHIN THE WORLD

Does the sufferer really care? They surely have read that the whole world lies in (the power of) the evil one? (1 John 5:19), that friendship with the world is enmity with God? (James 4:4), and that the world will hate Christians because it first hated Jesus (John 15:18)? They have already made their decision to come out of darkness into light (1 John 1:6-7), to renounce antichrist and follow the Lord, or they would not or should not be receiving your ministry.

The world appears at the moment less likely to oppose deliverance than some sections of the Christian church, but nevertheless sufferers can expect opposition from non-Christians, as the Lord has warned.

(ii) OPPOSITION WITHIN THE CHURCH

Many Christians are "naturally" reluctant to take on satan's hosts in frontal attack. They are happy to rest passively in Christ's victory nineteen centuries ago and look for an easier way to lead a "triumphant" life, in preference to getting involved in deliverance. Unfortunately this is not much help to the sea of suffering humanity around us. The minister rather than the sufferer will receive most of the uninformed criticism, but it is highly probable that well-meaning Christians will endeavour to persuade the sufferer that everything is really quite alright - they don't need deliverance (much). They are told to walk in the Spirit, control the desires of the flesh, overcome sin etc. etc.. Such limited counsel often comes from people who do not understand the relationship between **sin,** the **flesh,** the **world** and **demons.** Other counsellors will advise a sufferer to stop imagining things and they will feel much better tomorrow after a couple of disprins and a good night's sleep - such is the quality of advice received by some tormented people. It can be likened to applying a band-aid to an amputation - inadequate and temporary to say the least.

I would like to now share with you a prophetic message which came from the Lord during a Deliverance and Restoration meeting in 1986:

> THUS SAITH THE LORD: TRULY WHAT I HAVE IN STORE FOR YOU IS FAR GREATER THAN YOU CAN IMAGINE OR THINK. THE RESTORATION THAT IS MY PURPOSE TO DO IN YOUR LIVES TRANSCENDS ANYTHING THAT YOU COULD CONCEIVE IN YOUR MIND OF FLESH, BUT AS YOU CONTINUE IN MY WORD AND AS YOU CONTINUE TO BE LED BY MY SPIRIT SO YOU *WILL* BEGIN TO PERCEIVE WHAT I PURPOSE TO DO. YOU WILL *BEGIN* TO *CATCH* THE *VISION* OF WHAT YOU ARE TO BE. STEP BY STEP YOU WILL MOVE INTO, BEING TRANSFORMED INTO, THE NEW CREATURE WHICH TRULY IS IN THE IMAGE OF MY SON.

THERE WILL BE THOSE WHO DO NOT UNDERSTAND MY PURPOSES, BROTHERS AND SISTERS OF YOURS IN MY SON JESUS; BRETHREN WHO HAVE NOT YET CAUGHT ANY PART OF MY RESTORATIVE PURPOSES. AND THEY WILL SEEK TO HOLD YOU IN BONDAGE, NOT DELIBER-ATELY, BUT BECAUSE THEY HAVE NOT RECEIVED WHAT MY SPIRIT IS SAYING TO THE CHURCHES.

AND AS MY SPIRIT SPEAKS TO THE CHURCHES, SO THERE WILL BE MANY WHO WILL FOLLOW IN YOUR FOOTSTEPS; WHO *WILL* CATCH THE VISION; WHO *WILL* DESIRE *HUNGRILY* TO *MOVE* INTO IT; WHO WILL MAKE GREAT *STRIDES* INTO THE THINGS OF THE SPIRIT AND WHO WILL NOT LISTEN TO THOSE WHO, ALTHOUGH WELL-MEANING, *ARE BLIND GUIDES;* WHO SAY THEY SEE BUT ARE BLIND. FOR THEY CAN ONLY SEE AS MY SPIRIT OPENS THEIR EYES, AND MY SPIRIT WILL OPEN THE EYES OF THOSE WHO SEEK THE LORD IN ALL HIS FULL-NESS. FOR IT *IS* THE LORD WHO IS THE SPIRIT; WHO WILL GIVE *SIGHT* TO THE BLIND ENABLING THEM TO SEE THE THINGS WHICH KINGS AND PROPHETS LONGED TO SEE BEFOREHAND.

THERFFORE, TAKE NO I IEED TO THOSE WHO *ARE BLIND GUIDES;* DISMISS THEIR WORDS FOR THEY WILL NOT HELP YOU. CATCH THE VISION YOURSELVES; SEEK *ME;* ASK ME BY MY SPIRIT TO GIVE YOU SIGHT, AND STEP BY STEP ALL THINGS WILL BE UNFOLDED FOR YOU FOR MY SPIRIT TRULY IS ABLE TO LEAD YOU INTO ALL TRUTH AS YOU MAKE YOURSELVES AVAILABLE TO RECEIVE.

Talking your problems out with a counsellor may be another

form of band-aid. There are some problems that can be helped enormously by sitting down and talking with an experienced counsellor, but if the problem is inspired by the presence of an unclean spirit then, notwithstanding the fact that talking things out may give an encouraging lift to the human spirit, the spiritual problem in the soul will quickly re-assert itself and the sufferer will be back at square one again. If the problem is spiritual or even possibly spiritual **any attempt to talk the sufferer out of deliverance is not of the Lord.** Unfortunately the church has had its share of blind guides, indeed all teachers make many mistakes (James 3:1-2), but in the timing of the Lord the spiritual warfare is in much sharper focus today and becoming clearer all the time to those who have teachable hearts.

(iii) OPPOSITION WITHIN THEMSELVES

(a) Understanding Emotions

We have indicated that most healing and/or deliverance is progressive for a variety of reasons and some folk make dramatic progress from the beginning with hardly any obstacles. They not only get better and know it, but they feel it too. However should they become overconfident and think that spiritual warfare is easy they will be in for a rude awakening unless you prepare them for the counter-attack of the enemy. The feelings and emotional ups and downs are illustrated in graph form by Case History "A".

Please notice that Ministry relieves the pressures, which then build up until the next deliverance session. If the sufferer is not prepared for the slump in well-being when the enemy comes back at them like a flood, they could easily give up the fight and thus remain bound in spiritual chains for the rest of their life, never attaining their potential for

"FEELINGS"
CASE HISTORY "A"

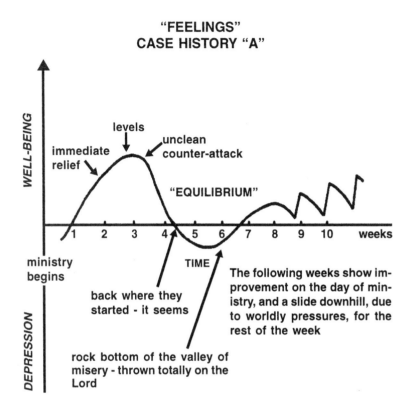

Christ. However it should be remembered that Case History "A" depicts FEELINGS, WHICH MAY HAVE NO RELATIONSHIP TO THE REAL PROGRESS being achieved in the cleansing of the soul.

Some other sufferers do not even know the encouragement of feeling better at the beginning but are immediately plunged into heavy spiritual and emotional warfare. They are getting better in reality but feel worse for a season. This is often true of people with particularly heavy "mind control" problems such as paranoia and/or schizophrenia.

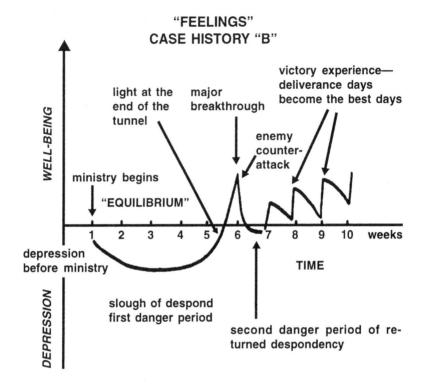

"FEELINGS"
CASE HISTORY "B"

Case History "B" shows a fairly consistent pattern of an improving emotional state, after an initial very difficult period. It is SO IMPORTANT that the sufferer be encouraged and upheld by every possible means when in the long black tunnel of despair. They WILL win if they TRUST and hang onto the Lord Jesus, but ignorance of what is really happening at this point can be very damaging to one's morale.

It is the people who suffer in this way, whose FEELINGS get worse instead of better from the very beginning who are least likely to continue receiving ministry. A conviction from the Holy Spirit, and a "knowing" that they can trust their ministers with their life is necessary if they are to obtain victory. Without these two essentials the sufferer will give up and take away with them a very poor testimony. Other sympathetic Christians will be told that, "Mary went to Full Salvation Fellowship for deliverance but she got worse instead of better!" The ministry, not the devil, will get the blame, and satan will have won a great victory. He has been able to

1. Stop the ministry to the sufferer.
2. Pass the blame onto a genuine ministry of the Lord by slander and ignorance.
3. Effectively prevent others in great need from seeking help.
4. Impugn the honour and the glory of the Lord, in whose Name we minister.

Is it any wonder that we like to at least have contact with people very briefly and examine their motivation before ministering, whenever possible?

It is also an opportunity for informing, encouraging and preparing the sufferer. I have encouraged the people in our Deliverance and Restoration program to share what God is doing for them, and after their witnessing invite other Christians to come to our meetings. When someone accepts their invitation we now request our regulars **they** prepare the new person for what to expect, because we simply don't have the time or opportunity.

Please remember that in PROGRESSIVE deliverance, where we are not just removing the tip of the iceberg, but attacking and removing the invisible bulk of danger below the surface of a sufferer's personality, just about EVERYONE will experience a valley of misery (Ps. 84:6) sooner or later. Many will experience several but if they can hold onto the Lord and the victory promises in His Word at such

54

times, remembering all His promises and praising Him by faith, they CANNOT LOSE - they will indeed come into a well of blessing, provision and life in the Spirit.

It will not always be easy - they will be tested and tried but not beyond what they are able to bear (1 Cor. 10:13). A homosexual for example, knows that when he is converted to Jesus Christ the battle is not over but just beginning. Before his conversion, society could be blamed for all his feelings of guilt, frustration, loneliness, confusion, distortion and destructive anger. He could allow himself to be persuaded that "they" were responsible and that once "moral persecution" was eliminated, he could live happily ever after, doing his own thing in a pluralistic non-condemnatory society. However, when the Holy Spirit is invited in, his conscience is sensitised even further and battle flares within the soul. He discovers that his frustration and oppression does not come from without (society) but from *within himself* and in the majority of cases, conversion and the receiving of God's Spirit does not provide automatic deliverance and victory, neither does ongoing "normal" Christian involvement. Assurances that Jesus is sufficient for every need begin to have a rather hollow sound to them and doubt creeps in. The desperate choices that appear to lie before him are:

1. Admit failure as a Christian and fall back into the world.

2. Fight on by maintaining sexual celibacy, hopefully resisting the enormous pressure.[1]

---

[1] The Bible discusses a number of agencies opposing Christ from within the human body and a discussion of these areas, such as "sin", "the flesh", demons and "the old man" appears in **"Your Full Salvation"** and Book 4 **"Discerning Human Nature"** by the same writer. All these areas of a human being will oppose deliverance, and teaching is the key to providing ALL the spiritual weapons from the scriptures in order to obtain CONTINUING victory.

3.   Join a "Christian" church where homosexuality is not regarded as a sin but as an expression of love.

If he is faithful to New Testament teaching, choice 3 is automatically eliminated as a blind alley to hell, and if he finds his dark urges becoming overwhelmingly and agonisingly dominant choice 2 becomes "impossible," leaving choice 1 as the only apparent alternative.

The only alternative? Thank God the answer is NO! For all the promises of God are YES in Christ (2 Cor. 1:20). Jesus is the Great Deliverer - praise the Lord - and not only for sexual problems, but for those who are fearful, confused, violent, bitter, sorrowful, rejected, unloved, arrogant, domineering, greedy, cursed by the occult and crushed in spirit. Indeed, our Lord Jesus Christ bled and died on the Cross to set us all free from EVERY kind of bondage (Matt. 8:16-17. 1 John 3:8).

(b)   Assessing Progress

Sharing the victories we can have in Christ leads me to make a few comments about how we can ASSESS THE PROGRESS that a sufferer has made, and to do this I would like to illustrate diagrammatically the human soul in the form of a jar.

At conversion the Holy Spirit enters the soul (jar) and like clean, living water He brings life to the beleaguered human spirit. Although the mud gets stirred up and perhaps some of it is eliminated, the main benefit is that the human spirit is brought from a "death" situation to life. It experiences the new birth or being BORN AGAIN or ANEW and it is no longer *drowning* in uncleanness. If the new Christian then experiences a second blessing or a pouring out of the Holy Spirit upon him to the point where the measure can be described as a FILLING, then the jar is filled to overflowing and because of this overflowing a great deal of mud and little stones will be stirred up and caught up and carried up over the brim of the jar (soul) and removed forever - praise the Lord! This substantially reduces the amount of uncleanness within the jar (soul).

Before Conversion

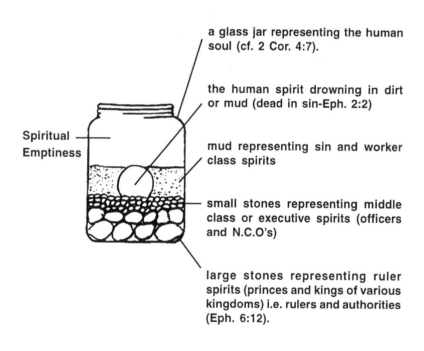

a glass jar representing the human soul (cf. 2 Cor. 4:7).

the human spirit drowning in dirt or mud (dead in sin-Eph. 2:2)

Spiritual Emptiness

mud representing sin and worker class spirits

small stones representing middle class or executive spirits (officers and N.C.O's)

large stones representing ruler spirits (princes and kings of various kingdoms) i.e. rulers and authorities (Eph. 6:12).

HOWEVER, MANY SMALL STONES AND NEARLY ALL THE LARGE STONES WILL REMAIN. THEY WILL NOT SHIFT THEIR GROUND UNTIL THE WATER (HOLY SPIRIT) GETS UNDERNEATH THEM AND BEARS THEM UP AND THRUSTS THEM OUT OF THE JAR. This is where the ministry of deliverance specifically applies. It move。 what seeks to be immovable by the power of God and through the determined and consistent application of the ministry, in Jesus' Name!

Thus we can say that when people today claim to be filled with the Spirit they are really claiming to have been "topped up"[1] with the Spirit to the point of overflowing. Many stones - the "heavies" - remain, and so a person can be "filled with the Spirit" to the top, EVEN TO OVERFLOWING, and still need considerable deliverance. I am speaking about spiritual things in human, physical terms, of course, to make the point.

So how do we measure the progress a person is making? Well, one way of NOT assessing progress is by viewing the outward manifestation of demons leaving. Some people manifest very noisily or dramatically which sometimes leads to others, who get releases more quietly, thinking that the noisy ones are getting more or better or deeper deliverance, but this is not borne out by our experience.

We had a young man and a young woman receiving deliverance who, as it happened, were both receiving help from the same psychiatrist. Because of this "coincidence" they used to sit together in our meetings, but that is where the similarity ended. Over several months the girl would wail and scream and cry. The young man however showed no outward manifestation whatsoever, like the great majority of people. He would sit through every meeting quite wooden-faced, without any outward physical manifestation at all.

Both made good progress and one day reported with great

at the psychiatrist had, within the space of two
:h other, DISCHARGED BOTH OF THEM from
see him any further. Apparently the quiet suf-
_.... get free just as quickly as the noisy ones, if they
have the faith to trust God's Word and promises and believe
that HE IS doing in them what they have asked Him to do.

Why do so many people receive QUIET, even SILENT,
ministry while a small percentage experience noisy releases?

Here are two reasons:

(i)   You may remember from Book 2 "Engaging the En-
      emy" that in our meetings demons are COMMANDED
      to leave quickly, QUIETLY, and harmlessly. It is a vital
      part of the authoritative control Verlie and I exercise
      over the enemy during ministry, by the grace of God.
      We don't need a lot of noise to convince us that good
      things are happening.

(ii) There are many exits from the human body that de-
      mons can take. Nose, eyes, skin, anus, ears, scalp
      etc., but only one of them is noisy, and that is the
      MOUTH. Even then, yawning, hiccupping and some
      coughing are not necessarily noisy.

No, the extent of the manifestations is no measure at all.
How, then do we measure a sufferer's progress? It would
be easy to say "by their fruits", but for the deceptive battle
campaign waged by the powers of darkness, which means
that fruit of the Holy Spirit do not always come forth immediately, during battle, but WHEN THE BATTLE IS WON!
Peace in all its fulness flows AFTER the battle, or I should
say, after the WAR is over!

It would be easy to think that with the exit of so much

uncleanness, the fruit of the Holy Spirit should always be manifested more and more, and life should be one continuous stream of (easy) victories. Sometimes this is true - praise the Lord - but it is seldom so straightforward. We have seen that a person can be making really good progress but be feeling quite low and miserable, perhaps due to satan's favorite ploy of throwing **doubt**, **unbelief**, **fear** and **confusion** into the fray, and it is very difficult for a person suffering from confusion to be convinced that he or she is making very good progress.

All they know is that they are confused and don't know what to do next. Thus the problem is that **the judgment of people receiving deliverance is generally quite clouded and they are often unable to assess their own progress.** This is another very good reason why we really need to submit to the ministry of another person we can trust and not practice ministering to oneself, if at all possible.[1]

The minister, who has some idea of the muck that has come out, may need some kind of overall measure or yardstick of the progress made. So the question remains, HOW can we obtain some kind of idea of the progress achieved, bearing in mind that a person in the midst of continuous deliverance may not ALWAYS be able to show forth the fruit of the Spirit of God as quickly as we would wish?

When accurate measuring of a sufferer's progress is important (and only then) the answer is that continuous ministry, i.e. continuous stirring up of the mud, could cease for a season. The battle could be allowed to simmer right down so that THE PRESENT TRUE STATE OF THE SOUL CAN BE COMPARED WITH THE ORIGINAL STATE OF THE

---

[1] Book 2, Chapter 5.9

60

SUFFERER. Assessment can only be made with any accuracy by comparing the condition existing in the sufferer BEFORE and AFTER seasons of ministry have been completed, so it may be desirable to plan short seasonal breaks in the ministry, such as Christmas and New Year etc.[1] with their families, thus allowing the battle in the soul to subside and settle down. This is also important because IT IS ONLY WHEN THE SOUL IS SETTLED THAT THE SUFFERER experiences the BENEFITS of the ministry to the full. The mud and stones settle because the ministry of the Holy Spirit ceases to stir, and so we do not have uncleanness constantly surfacing in the personality to the same extent, and as a result of that, the fruit of the Holy Spirit can emerge and manifest. At this point the sufferer will probably look and feel better than they have ever felt in their lives before, and will be a source of great joy to the minister, obtaining great pleasure from briefly remembering the original miserable state of the sufferer manifested at the first contact, some time before.

Of course, as soon as the ministry group resumes and your sufferer again continues to receive ministry, then the spiritual mud and stones will be stirred up afresh and surface in the personality and an ongoing accurate assessment of progress made may again become almost impossible. Obviously the sufferer must keep clearly in mind the vision of what Christ wants to complete in them, otherwise they may settle for a second - best level of blessing and not return to the ministry after a break.

So what I am saying is—when you want to measure progress, let *the mud and muck settle.* The "new" person

[1] We now conduct ministry programs of three terms a year, totalling 40 weeks of ministry. This allows 12 weeks of "normalising", as well as missions, conferences and refreshment.

can then be compared with the old, and in many cases you may have to briefly remind your sufferers just how bad their condition once was. This is not a matter of condemnation, negativity or looking backwards but simply clearly seeing what the Lord has done and giving Him thanks and praise!

(c) Ensuring a Good Testimony

It is not much use the minister alone seeing the progress but IT IS VITAL THAT THE SUFFERER BE MADE TO SEE AND BE AWARE OF THE PROGRESS THEY HAVE MADE. This is tremendously encouraging to them and enables them to thank and praise and give glory to God from a full heart as well as to testify to others of His delivering grace and encourage others to receive ministry also. For this reason I STRONGLY ENCOURAGE A SUFFERER TO COMMIT HIMSELF OR HERSELF FOR A MINIMUM OF TEN (10) SESSIONS OVER A TERM OF THIRTEEN WEEKS. This enables NOTICEABLE improvement to be made and gives the sufferer something to praise God positively about, rather than risk a miserable, negative confession that, "Nothing much happened. If anything I feel worse!" - after one or two sessions. Satan loves to make capital out of the impatience, ignorance and unbelief of Christians, but we can defeat this ploy from the outset, by the grace and wisdom of God. Once improvement has been recognised, the sufferer can be encouraged to press on into even greater freedom and Christlikeness.

(d) Soulish Warfare

You will remember that in the last chapter under the heading "Battle Tactics of the Enemy", we mentioned the **Deliverance Cycle** and the severity of opposition to the deliverance ministry that can rise from within the human soul, i.e. the sufferer's emotions. Let us assume, for example, that a person with lust spirits has begun receiving ministry from you. Very often there is an immediate reduction in unclean desires and both you and the sufferer can praise God for the encouraging initial improvement.

Lapses

However, as the weaker spirits are removed and stronger ones engaged in battle, the sufferer begins to complain of extremely lustful pressures. There may be a lapse in their moral behaviour and they may be filled with guilt, and you with disappointment. However, DO NOT CAST THEM OFF. If repentance is expressed, forgive and continue the ministry. Remember the seventy times seven and the long-suffering grace of God that abounds far more than your own impatience. Be led by the Holy Spirit, not by your own rules and regulations. There may come a time when you are convicted that someone loves their sin too much to let it go and you may have to let THEM go, with the sin they love, but while they express a GENUINE desire to be free of their bondage, repent, and continue fighting, then the man or woman of God should fight shoulder to shoulder with them until victory is achieved.

Deceptive Feelings

You will remember we said that the sufferer will have to overcome spirits of fear, unbelief, confusion and other mind-control spirits. To illustrate, I remember a young married couple coming to me after having come to our meetings for several months and the young man was unhappy with his spiritual condition.

"Peter", he said, "I don't seem to be making any progress -

I don't feel very good at all - what's wrong?" So I dug out of my confidential file the personal details of his life, which he had given me when he first came to us for help.

"Well", I asked, "have you still got that terrible jealously when your wife talks to another man?" "No", he said, "that seems to gave gone." "Have you still got that violent streak in you that causes you to strike her?" "No", he said, looking, a little brighter, "I haven't hit her for ages." "Do you still get angry with her?" "No..." He was beginning to look positively cheerful at this point "Hey, I'm glad I came and talked to you. I didn't realise how much progress I had made!" We went through another half-dozen spiritual problems which the young man had complained of when he first came to us and they had all virtually disappeared, BUT the Holy Spirit had continued to search him out in the innermost parts of his being, and NOW he was manifesting a whole new range of problems which he didn't even know he had. If we had not been able to compare his earlier condition (from our records) with his present experience the evil one would have been able to convince him that the ministry was no good, he was wasting his time and, in fact, he was (felt) worse, not better. He would have left the ministry and taken away with him a miserable testimony which satan would have been able to use to discourage others, and the Lord would have received no thanksgiving or glory, which is His due.

I share this account with you because it is not an uncommon situation and recurs regularly. It not only underlines some of the enemy's battle tactics which have deceived many in the past (and, unfortunately, will endeavor to do so in the future), but it illustrates the truth that there is a WIDE RANGE of spiritual problems in the children of God, most of whom are almost completely unaware of the true situation within them.

64

Not only is the "average" Christian unaware but so also many of the pastors. Consequently, when someone does go from our deliverance meetings, muttering under their breath, "I don't like that ministry, let me get out of there - it didn't do me any good - I feel WORSE" and they take their testimony back to their home church or another ministry, very few Christian leaders are able to discern that they are listening to the unclean testimony of spirits of unbelief, confusion, mind-control, hatred, destruction, paranoia and schizophrenia etc., NOT the human spirit, NOR the Holy Spirit of Truth.

Even anointed Pentecostal or charismatic ministers are sometimes deceived by the subtlety of the powers of darkness. They will readily believe everything the enemy says through the mouth of a sufferer as gospel truth, not understanding the deception of the enemy, partly because, too often, what is in THEM WANTS to hear criticism of other Christian ministries, especially powerfully anointed Christian ministries that are considered a threat to their own fleshly empire-building ambitions.

Always suspect that you are listening to an unclean spirit when you hear a Christian minister or ministry being criticised.

It MAY NOT be unclean if it is the truth spoken in love because of a Godly responsibility to so speak, but if the criticism is ill-informed (and so many of them are), at the very least it is unwise and uncharitable, and probably unclean.

The safest course is to NEVER be a party to criticism of another ministry about which you are not well informed after PERSONAL investigation.

The current move of the Holy Spirit known as **the Toronto**

blessing is a classic example of well-meaning but ill-informed criticism[1] being levelled at a true move of God, even though those involved don't seem to have a lot of answers at the time of writing. It is deliverance pioneers like **Dr. Derek Prince** who have got it right!

So we have the incredible, but predictable, situation where unclean spirits are being used to drive wedges between anointed ministries of Christ, especially where a deliverance ministry is involved, but I am encouraged by the Word of the Lord:

> **"So have no fear of them; for nothing is covered that will not be revealed, or hidden that will not be known. What I tell you in the dark utter in the light; and what you hear *whispered (in the ear) proclaim upon the housetops." (Matt. 10:26-27, See also 1 Cor. 4:5)***

All the fleshly, unclean corruption of the human heart will be laid bare and we shall all stand before the One who justifies and the One who condemns, He who sees the truth as it really is.

A spirit of **fear** being thrown up into the fray is another very common enemy ploy. A woman who visited our meeting said to me as she left, "All this coughing, spluttering and screaming - you've frightened the life out of me." To which I replied, as graciously as I could, "Not really, sister, we're frightening the death out of you."

Words Misunderstood

On another occasion a young man couldn't handle the

---

[1] See our publication **"Toronto and the Truths You Need to know"**.

meeting and wanted to leave early. "Sure", said **Verlie,** "I'll just get **Peter** and **Jack** to bind you up and you can go", meaning, of course, that Jack and I would pray with the young man and take further authority and bind up all the unclean spirits that were manifesting in him to be silent, inactive and harmless so that he could leave in peace, without harm to others or himself, until the next meeting.

"No one is binding me!", he shouted, and we realised that the spirit of **confusion** had twisted our words so that he thought we were literally going to bind him up physically with ropes or chains. Confusion really can make people get things back to front. One meeting when the Power of God was heavily upon the assembly, **Verlie** could see in the spirit what was happening and said to the people, "If you are feeling heavy, put yourself down on the carpet and let the Lord have His way with you." We wondered why one sister was fighting the Power of God but it became clear later when she said, "The Lord doesn't give His people a spirit of **heaviness** but a garment of praise (Isa. 61:3), so I wasn't going to receive that heaviness - I kept on praising Him!". This dear sister had resisted the flow of the Power of the Spirit of God, fighting the physical heaviness of the power, so that she could keep on singing praises! She had confused the beautiful physical "heaviness" that comes from the Lord during ministry with the spirit of heaviness in the soul, akin to being burdened in the emotions by forms of depression such as mourning and grieving, loneliness etc.

We have to be so careful with our choice of words when ministering deliverance, because if there are two possible interpretations of what we say, we may be sure that the enemy will seek to control the mind by imposing a deception upon the sufferer, who will already be under a great deal of internal, soulish pressure.

Symptoms

Why do the pressures become so great from within the soul? FIRSTLY, as we have already explained, the further the ministry progresses, the stronger the spirits encountered. SECONDLY and most importantly, it should be realised that spirits surfacing in the soul for removal will manifest their character before leaving. That is so important I want to say it again in different words - SPIRITS THAT ARE LEAVING WILL MANIFEST THEIR DESIRES IN AND THROUGH THE FLESH AS THEY SURFACE AND DEPART. What they crave the sufferer will crave; what they are, they will try to make the sufferer also. Some give the sufferer a lot of trouble on the way out. Why do they do this to a sufferer? It is simple really. THEY WANT TO STAY. They do not want to go, but the deliverance minister has commanded them to go and the Holy Spirit is enforcing the commands given in Jesus' Name. Thus, they only have ONE chance of avoiding eviction and that is to persuade their house (the sufferer) that he or she doesn't really want to be rid of them but, in fact, the sufferer should enjoy them and let them stay. So, the unclean spirit of lust that is being evicted, surfaces and does all that it can to pressure the sufferer into giving in to lustful desires and enjoying them. TO GIVE INTO THE UNCLEAN SPIRIT AND EXERCISE LUST IS TO PERMIT IT TO STAY, and even to invite others in. To abstain from fleshly lusts which war against the soul is to have victory over them and speed their removal and the sufferer's cleansing.

What does all this mean? It means that the sufferer MUST RESIST the demons when the pressure is on - and release will follow. The Word of God says **"Resist the devil and he will flee from you. Draw near to God and He will draw near to you."** (James 4:7-8). This demonic release can be speeded up by the well-proven practice of praising God. The sufferer may feel terrible, miserable, and under enormous pressure but let them RESIST THE DEMONS — COMMAND THEM TO GO in Jesus Name — and then DRAW NEAR TO GOD with praise and thanksgiving, confessing the wonderful works of God. No demon can stand such warfare and release will be obtained-normally quite quickly.

Some people suffering from depression or paranoid spirits may manifest by unfolding a great long tale of woe "Oh me, oh my, poor me!" But somehow they have to learn to praise God even if their teeth are gnashing and grinding with self pity and frustrated anger. *Their own spirit must rise up in Jesus Name and overrule the unclean spirit* that is trying to hold onto and dominate the house (sufferer).

Victory is the Christian's - in the Name of the Lord - but it must be TAKEN!

To put it yet another way it is very important that ALL SYMPTOMS experienced by a sufferer **after authoritative and anointed deliverance ministry has been applied** should be seen or interpreted as OUTWARD GOING junk or poison by the sufferer, NOT INCOMING junk. That is, symptoms MUST be understood as VICTORY battles and RELEASES and not a flood of the enemy overcoming them. We know from the Word of God that when unclean spirits were forced to leave at Jesus' command they often came out during convulsions (fitting) and screams (Mark 1:26). One dear elderly saint complained to me that since she had begun receiving deliverance ministry she kept wanting to spit out mucous. As she had a rather unfortunate, haughty, aristocratic style of speaking it always came across as a rebuke, as if I was to blame and should do something about it. Having explained the relationship between symptoms and releases for the umpteenth time I finally said to her, "You ought to thank God for the mildness of your symptoms. Perhaps you would rather be dashed to the ground, and convulsed and froth at the mouth like the young lad in the Bible!" (Mark 9:20,26). Needless to say I wasn't very popular but the point got through.

You can see therefore that the sufferer's attitude to, and interpretation of, symptoms in the flesh will dictate their practical responses. We can grizzle, gripe and whine or we can praise the Lord with truly thankful hearts for what He is doing. Which response do you think is the response of faith and pleasing to the Lord? It is therefore **vital to praise the Lord for symptoms** of infirmity in the flesh and not let the enemy's huffing and puffing deceive anyone into abandoning the Faith Position. Keep in mind that whingers and grizzlers get nothing from the Lord (James 1:8).

"But", they may say, "Is it not possible that I could get a fresh attack from OUTSIDE? How do I know that all my symptoms are the manifestation of outward going spiritual poison and not, for example, that I am catching the 'flu?"

Well, nobody can guarantee that one hundred percent but:

IF they have received anointed ministry, with proven discernment and power, and

IF they have followed the counselling, e.g. kept under the Blood of the Passover Lamb, and

IF they have not done anything foolish, such as standing in a draught half-dressed, and

IF they have truly held and believed the promises of God

THEN they can, and should, hold the Faith Position firm

until the battle has been decided in their favour. It is not as hard as it sounds!

When we have a ministry meeting which includes ministry against spirits of infirmity for example, we nearly always have a rash of 'flu symptoms with people complaining "I've caught the 'flu". But of course they have not caught a NEW batch of viruses but are simply being cleaned out of the old storehouse of infection locked into their bloodstream and organs. The only way this can be "proved" is by experiencing a reduction of bouts of 'flu in succeeding years. Improbable? Not at all. I would say this is the normal experience of those who have been with us over the longer term.

The response we make to our symptoms and our confession (what we say) are so important. Our conversation (spoken word) finds us out. (Ps. 37:30-31, Ps. 71:23-24) i.e. indicates what spirit/Spirit is ruling over our lives. In conclusion it may be said that if anyone receiving deliverance experiences the kind of pressures from within the soul that we have been discussing it is *genuinely a cause for joy and praise.* It means the enemy has surfaced, is fighting desperately, and the sufferer has only to stand fast in Christ and follow his/her minister's directions in order to enjoy the fruits and victory of release.

Now that you have read this brief section headed "Soulish Warfare" please go back to the beginning and read it again. It is one of the most important sections in this series of books.

(e) Letting Go!

1. *Unconscious Resistance*

At one Deliverance and Restoration meeting Verlie was

moving amongst the sufferers and ministering freely when I heard her say to one person "Let it go - don't hold back - let it all go!"

After the meeting this person spoke to me and said "How DO you let go? I wasn't aware of holding anything back and thought I was co-operating."

Unconscious resistance is not an uncommon problem for many people, especially those with a quiet, shy personality, or people who are sensitive to embarrassment. What happens is that without even realising it some folk "put on the brakes" inside them. They exercise a tight control and subconscious opposition to the ministry of the Holy Spirit and because of this their progress is very slow.

Because they are UNAWARE that they are fighting the ministry deep down inside them, they usually think they are co-operating and therefore will need the minister's help to understand they have tightened up inside, and perhaps seek to understand the reasons why.

Reasons:

Just about every reason is based on the FEAR of manifesting publicly in front of other people and making a fool of themselves. Deep inside them they experience one or more of the following fears, e.g.:

(i)   Fears for personal safety

One seriously afflicted person experienced the terrifying sensation of falling, falling, falling... into a black pit WHEN GOING THROUGH RELEASE. The natural (soulish) instinct was to strongly resist this ordeal and although the power of the risen Christ brought this person safely through each time the desperate inner resistance meant that progress was very slow. The answer, of course, was to trust the ministry of Christ Jesus and allow herself to fall into the blackness experience ("Yea, though I walk through the valley of the shadow of death I WILL FEAR NO EVIL"), knowing that Jesus was there with her in the blackness, but it is easier said than done. Faith (trust) when your very life seems to be at stake is the only way to turn defeat into victory, non-progress into progress, bondage into release.

(ii) Embarrassment that their unclean spirits may make a DRAMATIC departure, after so many have gone quietly. This is not uncommon for shy people who hope that their deliverance will be a private matter, even in a public meeting.

(iii) Our Pride is sometimes challenged when we live in fear that we will make a fool of ourselves and we care too much about what our brothers and sisters in the Lord will think of us.

Some folk are so proud that they do not even think it is possible for them to have an unclean spirit, and their reasons have nothing to do with Christian doctrine, although they may say and think it does.

(iv) Self-consciousness lies somewhere between embarrassment and pride. It involves fears that everybody is:

a) watching them
b) laughing at them
c) passing judgement on them, and
d) they really are making a fool of themselves and will lose face and the esteem of their brethren.

The result is that for any one or more of the above rea-sons, any manifestation that is observable to others is quenched sub-consciously (in the soul) and the ministry of the Holy Spirit is fought against without the awareness of the conscious mind (intellect).

2. Solutions

What can be done about this unconscious resistance? Well the FIRST thing that has to happen is the deliverance min-ister must advise the sufferer that they are resisting.

This can bring a protest from the sufferer because they may not be aware of their resistance. However MOST sin-cere sufferers will be able to SEARCH WITHIN THEM-SELVES and, perhaps reluctantly, agree with their minister fairly quickly. SECONDLY, they must then "take off the brakes" within them by the exercise of the will of their hu-man spirit, putting down any anxiety about what the peo-ple sitting around them are going to think about their mani-festations. They must RESOLVE in their will, in the spirit of their minds, to LOOSEN UP and LET GO and LET GOD do what He wants to do. It helps if a sufferer can determine that their deliverance, cleansing and restoration is SO IM-PORTANT to them that it outweighs ALL other considera-tions, and make the decision "Whatever it takes, Lord..."

This is truly *"overthrowing every reasoning, argument and every high thing"* that opposes them (2 Cor. 10:3-5). They shut out every thought and every anxiety about what other people will think, because in truth it really doesn't matter and again the truth is that other sufferers are too busy getting their own releases from the Lord to worry about what is going on around them.

THIRDLY, the physical action of consciously opening one's

74

mouth and breathing steadily in and out for a short season physically assists the spiritual situation and has a releasing effect.

If you conduct your Deliverance and Restoration meetings IN THE CONTEXT OF CONTINUOUS PRAISE AND WORSHIP, as Verlie and I do each week, then that is a magnificent way of keeping people "in the spirit/Spirit" while they are receiving deliverance ministry.

I think it is impossible (humanly speaking) for people to be "in the spirit", that is, keep their minds on the Lord Jesus[1] for any length of time without exercising a spiritual discipline, such as prayer or praise. Praise for example, will keep sufferers in fellowship with the Lord, and while they are in such spiritual communion with Him, they can receive whatever deliverance the Lord has ordained for them. On the other hand, if they try to keep their spirit focussed on Jesus by the operation of their MIND only, they will quickly descend into the flesh rather than be in the spirit, and the deliverance they receive will be greatly reduced.

Singing praises and worshipping the Lord is the easiest and most enjoyable way I know for sufferers to tune into the Spirit and get deliverance, helping them to overcome all embarrassment and fear. If the worship stops and deliverance becomes difficult, one can always resort to release through steady breathing for a short time.

FINALLY, every victory is obtained by faith in the promises of God, and without faith it is impossible to please the Lord (Heb. 11:6). The Psalmist went on to say *"I will fear no evil, FOR YOU ARE WITH ME. Your rod and your staff comfort me."* (Ps. 23:4)

[1] See Book 2 Chap. 5.1 (iii) **"Final Instructions"**.

So then, the key to all release is for the sufferer to operate the words of a well-known song of praise:

> "So forget about yourself, and concentrate on Him, and worship Him"

3. Conscious Resistance

It seems strange to suggest that you will almost certainly be asked to minister deliverance to people who will then proceed to hinder your ministry quite openly. They will usually be "strong-minded" people used to dominating others rather than submitting to the leadership of another. As described in earlier chapters[1] they will probably try to dictate to you how you should minister to them, and resist any kind of ministry that differs from their own preconceptions.

Another equally common form of conscious resistance, but again related to the notion that the sufferer knows better than the minister, is the matter of CHOOSING the spirits to be cast out. For example, nearly everybody would like to get rid of their **fear** and **terror** spirits but not many people want to get rid of their **domination** spirits.

Broadly speaking, Christians are happy to lose spirits which cause them to be subject to or dependent on others, or cause them distress or pain, or any that have the effect of giving them low self-esteem such as fear, terror, all kinds of infirmity, confusion etc. However they are not always happy to lose the uncleaness which enables them to control, influence or dominate others, such as selfishness, lust, greed, bitterness, deception and especially religious spirits. In fact it is very hard for some to even admit to these latter, but rather attempt to justify them.

---

[1] Book 1, Chap. 4,2; Book 2, Chap. 5.12; Book 3, Chap. 7.1

How often have we known someone to come running up and crying out for help, and want it RIGHT NOW because they say they are so distressed, but when some relief has been obtained and the Lord begins to put His finger on other areas of their life, they cannot run away fast enough. We are encouraged when people are released into a new freedom in the early part of their ministry but what we RE-ALLY want to see them move into is a TOTAL CLEANS-ING PROGRAM in accordance with the command of the Lord (1 John 3:3). The question comes down to whether the sufferers WANT WHAT SUITS THEM[1] or WHAT THE LORD WANTS for them.

What is the solution? I suggest that you teach, encourage, inspire and pray for them, that their vision be lifted higher. In the meantime, do not be anxious; do not allow yourself to be hindered by them but GO FORWARD with the improvers. **Move with the movers!**

Problem people are, first and foremost, the Lord's problem.

(f)   A Common Deception

Another quite common tactic of the enemy is to pass itself off as the Holy Spirit. There are many Christians who claim to be led by the Holy Spirit and to hear the voice of God, and there can be no doubt that the Holy Spirit indwells them. Where the doubt arises is whether it is the Holy Spirit that they hear every time (or most of the time) or an unclean spirit masquerading as the Holy Spirit. They, of course, seldom have any doubt. To them it is always the Holy Spirit but the brethren with whom they fellowship are

---

[1] See Book 2, Chap. 5.9 (iv).

not so sure. It is very difficult, indeed impossible, in the natural realm, to convince some Christians that the voice they hear and obey is an unclean, counterfeit spirit of deception, perhaps a religious spirit,[1] and only a loving, patient honesty with such a brother or sister, pointing out the fruit (quality of advice) of the voice in question, measured against the Word of God and the witness of the Holy Spirit through other Christians, can reveal the truth.

This kind of deceptive, counterfeit Christ often turns up in people receiving deliverance. Its form of attack runs something like this:- *"I am the Lord thy God* (such blasphemy!) *and I will deliver you. Do not look any more toward man - look only to me and I will set you free. There is no need for you to attend this ministry any longer."*

Subtle - isn't it? It would be beautiful if it was truly of the Lord, but the last line exposes it as a probable fraud. The delighted sufferer promptly ceases warfare and very often comes back in six months time, much the worse for wear and tear, asking, "What went wrong? I obeyed the voice of the Lord and things seemed better for awhile (as things settled down) but now I'm worse than ever."

When we read the New Testament we find that deliverance is always ministered through the agency of a servant of God. Even the Lord Jesus (the Son of Man) ministered as His Heavenly Father directed Him. Only **king Nebuchadnezzer** in the Old Testament was possibly delivered directly from God without any *reported* human agency (Dan. 4:24-37). It is not that the Lord CANNOT act directly without a human agency, but rather that He has chosen to operate through the Church, the Body of Christ, so that we can

[1] Religious spirits will be more fully discussed in Book 4

enjoy the privilege of being co-workers with Him (1 Cor. 3:9 etc). To this end when He ascended on High He gave (spiritual) gifts to men (Eph. 4:7-8) that the Body members might care for each other and do greater works than even the Lord Jesus did whilst ministering on earth (John 14:12) - bearing in mind that the greater works that we do today ARE the works of the Lord Jesus through us, for we can do nothing without Him (John 15:5). For the unclean spirit to say "look only to me, not man" is crafty because that is exactly what the Lord through the deliverance minister says also. If the sufferer is looking to man, nothing lasting can be accomplished, but the Lord is not robbed of His glory when His people minister deliverance, or any other ministry, by the power of the Holy Spirit. The bottom line, "there is no need to attend ministry any more" exposes the motivation and its source. Only satan is interested in stopping deliverance and he hates it for it dispossesses him and reminds him that he is not really God after all.

The truth is that we are to look only to Jesus, not men, for His salvation, and to do this we turn to His servants, His ministers, in order that the Lord may minister to us through them according to their gifts from God. We can thank and appreciate His servants but we reserve all the glory and the praise for the Lord alone! Amen? It is indeed unusual for the Lord to minister deliverance directly, without using other members of His Body, and it is even rarer for Him to remove a sufferer from an effective ministry to do so, but of course, if people insist it is the direction of the Lord to them there is nothing more to be said. They have "pulled rank" on you and over - ridden your authority to minister to them by claiming the authority of the Most High. The only thing you can do (apart from the normal avenue of prayer) is pull right out of the situation, but leave the door open for their return should they discover they have erred. Time will tell, or, I should say, the Lord will reveal the true situation in the course of time to those with discernment.

8.2   OPPOSITION TO THE MINISTER

I think I have already hinted fairly strongly that the Christian leader who ministers deliverance is going to face plenty of opposition. We should not be surprised at this (although the vigour and savagery of it at times may surprise us) for did not our Lord Jesus warn us of this when He said *"If the world hates you, you know that it hated me before you... They shall put you out of the synagogues: yes, the hour comes that whoever kills you shall think that he offers service to God"* **(John 16:2).** If the world and the church of the day (religious spirits again?) resisted Jesus' ministry, do you doubt that they will resist the ministry of His disciples also? (John 15:18).

I once received a letter from a man in Sydney who regularly wrote anti-christian letters to the Press. He attacked me over the deliverance ministry and his complaint was that in casting out hundreds of unclean spirits every week we were making them homeless. "What are they going to do?" - was his plaintive cry of sympathy for them. It was easy to understand why he was an enemy of Christianity, and his attitude was not untypical of the world although he had a better (demonic) understanding of spiritual things than most citizens outside of the Christian faith. You may remember that when we were discussing the basic problem in the first chapter of Book 1 regarding the scope or need of the ministry, all kinds of objections such as the charge of being "demon - happy" and extremism were touched upon and the most common appeal was for *"moderation"* and *"balance"*. Unfortunately *"moderation"* and *"balance"* are variable products of the mind of man and therefore subject to his ignorance. How much better it would be If the cry went up "TRUTH! TRUTH! We march with God's Word in Spirit and in Truth and let the consequences fall where they may!" Unclean spirits are anything but moderate - they do not wage a "fair" warfare but one of lies, deceit and destruction; and how hypocritical it is to appeal for balance when the unclean spirits inhabiting the world have had it all their own way with hardly a Christian challenge since the apostolic age; and even 30 years ago you could probably count the Christians ministering deliverance regularly to the sea of sufferers in the State of New South Wales on your fingers and toes. Is that balance? The balance has been all satan's way, but that is coming to an end. We are talking about a SALVATION ministry - we are talking about the cleansing of the lives and souls of blood-bought Christians and where the needs of God's people are, there you will find a man or woman of God endeavouring to meet those needs. THAT IS GOD'S BALANCE! I think it is safe to say that the deliverance ministry was one of the **three** most provocative things that the Lord Jesus carried out regularly during His earthly ministry. Nothing so stirred up the Jews against Him as His persistent ministry on the **Sabbath,** His **teaching** and the **casting out of demons.** Theologians generally hate having their theology seriously challenged, let alone coming under full-scale assault such as Jesus brought to bear on the religious leaders of New Testament times. A great deal of profit can be gained by looking at the reactions to deliverance (casting out demons) in the New Testament as the Word of God will surely prepare us for the same reactions today in this twentieth century. Let us look at both the reaction of the world and the reaction of the church.

(i)   REACTION OF THE WORLD

Commercial Interests (in Gentile Philippi, representing the unbelieving World.)

"As we were going to the place of prayer, we were met by a slave girl who had a spirit of divination and brought her owners much gain by soothsaying" (Acts 16:16 R.S.V.).

As with "Opposition to the Sufferer" (8.1 (i)) it is no secret to Christians that *the whole world lies in the power of the evil one (1 John 5:19),* and that *friendship with the world is enmity with God (James 4:4).* Therefore it will not surprise you that when the light of Christ shines into worldly structures of commerce and entertainment etc. it is going to provide a better way - a true way of escape for the struggling pilgrim of life.

When people are soundly converted to Christ it affects their families, the kind of jobs they are prepared to do and the kind of entertainment they are prepared to receive - indeed their conversation and conduct at every level. Likewise with the salvation ministry of deliverance. It will often cut across commercial, political and emotional interests, and the incident of Paul's clash with the girl who had a **spirit of divination** (literally, the **spirit of a python**) is a good example. When the spirit had been cast out by the Apostle the girl could no longer divine the future, and her employers, frustrated at their loss of income, turned on **Paul** and **Silas**. After a fuss, including physical beating by the mob and the authorities, they were jailed (Acts 16:16-24).

One may have thought that the girl being delivered of an unclean python spirit was a cause for congratulations and joy but the attitude of the world was just the opposite. The loss of income was far more important than the girl's spiritual health and well-being. This same attitude reflecting the worship of the **god of economics** is also found amongst the silversmiths who made and sold objects representing the goddess **Artemis of the Ephesians.** Idolatry can appear very profitable in the short term (Acts 19:23f).

The truth of the matter is that the world is mainly interested in making money (1 Tim. 6:10), the more the better, and satan is very happy to make the purveyors of **drugs, prostitution** and **pornography** etc. very rich indeed (they obviously think they can take their riches with them), because his unclean spirits can then find plenty of access into human beings who pursue such unclean activities.

Amoral and permissively oriented **political parties** would be angered to have their policies widely exposed as unclean and creating a demons picnic, and this may easily happen in this generation. Some **liberal "Christians"** are going to be upset by this ministry because it verifies the truth of the Bible and shatters a variety of modern theological theories. It certainly creates immense problems for **agnostics, atheists** and orthodox non-Christian **psychiatry.** The reason psychiatry has so much influence in our lives is because the historic church has abdicated from its full responsibilities. I do not blame psychiatrists for being what they are or for their field of activity; they are simply trying to fill a gap that the church has created by its impotency and withdrawal. The word **"psychiatrist"** as you probably know, comes from two words, the word "psyche" meaning "soul" and "iatros" meaning "doctor", and so in its root meaning it means **"soul-doctor"**. Now as far as I understand the New Testament and indeed the Bible, it is the man of God who is a soul-doctor because his God is Maker, Repairer, Cleanser and Saviour of the soul, and when the church abdicated from its role, its spiritual role of helping people who are emotionally or mentally distressed, naturally enough medical scientists stepped in to endeavor to fill the gap, and who can blame them? I suggest that the ministry of deliverance effectively undermines all non-Christian attitudes and I would hope and pray that we will see the rise of a new dimension, that of Christian psychiatrists who will stand alongside the deliverance minister in their field of spiritual endeavour and together take on the forces of darkness in the name of Jesus Christ.

There are encouraging signs that some Christian psychiatrists are able, under the guidance of the Holy Spirit, to reconcile Biblical truth and their scientific training and thus offer an infinitely more effective ministry to their clients.

The Apostle's response to opposition from the world.

While it is doubtful if the apostles' response could have been anything more than desperate prayer while blows were raining on them, we do know that later in jail they were praying and praising God in accordance with their policy of praising God for everything. (Acts 16:25, 1 Thess. 5:16-18).

(ii) REACTION OF THE CHURCH

(a) The Multitudes (Jews)

And they were astonished beyond measure, saying, "He has done all things well; he even makes the deaf hear and the dumb speak." (Mark 7:37 R.S.V.)

I thank God for the multitudes and the crowds during Jesus' time on earth and I thank God for the grass roots of the Church today, because it is here that we see the greatest response of open-mindedness, open-heartedness and faith, childlike faith in the plain Word of God.

Church-going people today are generally amazed and impressed with successful healing and deliverance ministries. In the scriptures the crowds were amazed and said

"He does all things well" and they praised and magnified God for the ministry of Jesus as did the crowds in the early days of the Apostles. I thank God for "ordinary" believers. **However, crowd reactions can vary a great deal** depending on the character, understanding and open-mindedness of the individuals that make up the crowds. "Ordinary" churchgoing people normally do not have a great deal of theological understanding, so when God moves in a controversial way it is perhaps easier for them to apply their basic faith to what they see and hear, and to believe the plain Word of God because they see the heart of the matter, un-clouded by many and various philosophical and traditional considerations. They can say like the ex-blind man answering the Jews about Jesus *"Whether he is a sinner, I do not know,* **one thing I know, that though I was blind, now I see!"** (John 9:25). For all of his miraculous power, the devil does not give sight to the blind to the glory of God! Crowds may be amazed and impressed with successful and authoritative ministry (Mark 1:27-28 etc.) or they may be unbelieving and perverse (Luke 9:41, Mark 9:26) depending on their prejudices and pre-disposition. **John the Baptist** even told the crowds they were snakey (Luke 3:7), a very helpful insight for ALL ministers of God's Word.

Jesus' response to such reactions.

He is plainly disgusted with unbelief and perversity, but while it is clear from scripture that faith is an essential response to His ministry and that unbelief prevented Him from achieving more (Mark 6:6), where there is a confusion and both faith and unbelief are present, Christ can act victoriously upon a sincere appeal for help (Mark 9:24).

(b) Friends and/or Relatives

There is an old expression which one jokes with close

friends. *"With you for a friend, who needs enemies"?* The Lord had "friends" like this during His earthly ministry. Concerned, well-meaning but blind and without understanding, they tried to interfere with the Lord's ministry and indeed, to stop Him:

> **Then He went into a house, and the crowd came together, so that they were not able to eat bread. And those with him (relations, friends) came forward to seize him, for they said 'He is beside himself'." (Mark 3:20-21)**

This incident took place in the context of the Pharisees charge of Beelzebub against Jesus, and a comparison with Matthew's record of this incident (Matt. 12:22-32) shows that it took place after the dramatic healing/deliverance of a blind and dumb demoniac.

Jesus clearly teaches that a prophet has no honour in his own house or country, because familiarity destroys objective perception, and it is therefore unlikely that friends and relatives can appreciate the truth when God raises up an anointed ministry in their own backyard. The anointed one is more likely to be seized and accused of paranoia by loved ones and committed for psychiatric observation. The deliverance minister would be wise to normally expect a strong and unfavourable reaction from his or her immediate family.

(c)   Religious Scholars

One of the most scandalous incidents recorded in the New Testament is that of the deliverance of an old Jewish woman from a **spirit of infirmity** in the Synagogue on the Sabbath Day (Luke 13:10-17). This mighty miracle was challenged by the Ruler of the Synagogue who questioned its lawfulness because it took place on the Sabbath. This important

86

man, for all his learning, did not understand the salvation and mercy of God, and was put to shame. We need not think that such legalistic, blind and merciless attitudes do not manifest themselves today - they have done, and still do—incredible but true.

I am sorry to say that some church leadership today would seem to make the Ruler of the Synagogue look like a saint. His shame was that he sought to squash deliverance and healing on the Sabbath, i.e., for only **one day in the week** (Luke 13:10-17). Compare his position and shame before the Lord with those who have either sought to squash the Lord's delivering grace right out of their denomination **seven days a week,** or reluctantly acknowledge the deliverance ministry purely as a Public Relations exercise in order to deceive the trusting church denominational membership, and outwardly keep up appearances as a Bible-believing Christian organisation.

I would like to emphasise that there is absolutely no need to fear or be in awe of such religious leaders or scholars. It does not matter how academic or important they have been or are, or how many University degrees they hold, because when it comes to the ministry of deliverance most of them would not know the presence of an unclean spirit if they tripped over it. They live and move amongst bound-up, demonised people every day. They counsel them, teach them, fellowship with them, apply their spiritual band-aids to them with well-meaning Christian conscientiousness. They trip over unclean spirits every day (metaphorically) **but they see nothing.**

Worse, and sad to say, many of them would not know even the person of the Holy Spirit if they confronted HIM, because it is an undeniable fact that He has been trying to break into the historic denominations for more than thirty years.

First the Holy Spirit manifestation of **tongues** was resisted, then **healing,** then **prophecy,** then **deliverance.** How many of you (readers) have been to a normal denominational service and have heard a prophetic word from the Lord allowed to come forth? Unfortunately not many at the time of writing. Some traditions cannot distinguish between **preaching** and **prophesying**[1] so what "chance" do they have? If they cannot discern the different manifestations of the HOLY Spirit who WANTS to be recognized as the Lord who is present, how can they perceive the often subtle and devious manifestations of unclean spirits in their midst? The wife of a minister friend of mine made us laugh the other day when she said "Peter, I used to think you were a bit way-out with the deliverance ministry and I accused you of seeing demons under every stone, but now I'm beginning to see them myself!" So dear brothers and sisters in Christ who hunger and thirst to be in the flow of God's great Restoration movement, do not be afraid or in awe of religious scholars but rather remember the Word of the Lord regarding them and leave them alone (Matt. 15:14).

The Bible also says that they themselves may have their share of unclean spirits (Gal. 4:9-10, Col. 2:8 R.S.V.) but they would probably be stunned and horrified if you told them so. I have in my library a cassette tape recording of *intellectual spirits* being cast out of someone who was described as having "an enquiring mind". It is a relic of the early days when I kept cassette recordings of the war against every type of spirit imaginable in the hope that they would help church leaders understand and accept the truth.

These particular **intellectual spirits came out screaming**

---

[1] It is interesting to note that this error of equating preaching and prophesying is being used by the ladies to lobby for the Ordination of women. Their banners quote the prophet Joel, "And your ... daughters will prophesy." -as evidence that they should preach **and teach.**

88

and I could not help but reflect how proud many people are of their brains, which are usually thought of as being a gift from God. Maybe they are a gift and may be they are not, it depends on the spirit that is using them. The vast majority of unclean spirits are not very bright, some are obviously stupid, but there are others which are very clever indeed and may well inspire prodigies and geniuses. Consider for example the life of **Wolfgang Mozart** (1756-1791 A.D.) presented to us through the film **"Amadeus".** The publicity for the film describes him as a coarse, bawdy drunkard, a screeching raucous child, **haunted by ghosts (spirits),** and the composer of the greatest music ever written. Has it not been said many times that genius is but a hairbreadth away from insanity? Child prodigies display skills and a maturity in their art form far in excess of their experience in this lifetime. Perhaps a reincarnated[1] unclean spirit with lifetimes of experience is the source of such amazing skills and maturity?

How much better it is to get the wisdom which is so freely available and which comes from above from the Father of lights, rather than the wisdom which is demonic (James 1:5-6,17:3:15).

Should we get into a debate or dispute with a very clever, demonised person who is presenting the lies of satan we can

(i)   use the wisdom which gave Peter and the apostles victory over the Religious Scholars opposing them (Acts 4:13-14), or if we are really up against it and are LED BY THE SPIRIT we might

(ii)   exercise our deliverance authority in Christ against the enemy (Acts 16:16-18).

---

[1] Please study "The Reincarnation Deception" in Book 4.

(iii) On one occasion the apostle Paul went even further than ministering deliverance and exercised the power of God with devastating effect against Elymas the sorcerer (Acts 13:6-12), however such awesome use of God's power should not be used unless BY THE CLEAREST LEADING OF THE HOLY SPIRIT!

It is a hard thing to say but Jesus said it and it needs saying again for this End-Time period. Jesus said the Religious scholars of His day were the offspring of vipers (Matt. 12:24,34), knowing that they were more interested in Church politics and advancing their own status and influence, both on a party and a personal basis. Now it is manifestly clear that Jesus was not talking of their PHYSICAL nature, for they were in the form of men. No, He was talking of their SPIRITUAL nature (within the SOULISH area, which includes the MIND), and any experienced deliverance minister will tell you that once the Lord begins digging into the souls of sufferers, it is not unusual for **snake spirits** to manifest themselves (cf. Acts 16:16, lit. the spirit of a python).

I don't need to add that whatever you say to any Christian brother or sister should be said in love and with Godly motives. If your motives are not right (i.e., your spirit is unclean) don't say anything until they are and even then beware the warning of the Lord not to cast your pearls before swine (Matt. 7:6). The **dog (wolf)** and **hog families of spirits** can be as destructive as the snake variety.

To put it very plainly the problem with Religious Scholars is that they are both religious and intellectual, and both these characteristics encourage personal pride and domination of others, which is another way of saying that they are usually bound up with **religious, intellectual** and **proud** spirits, even if they have been born again and have received the Holy Spirit.

They usually fear, or at least are uncomfortable with, the super-natural activities of the Holy Spirit (1 Cor. 4:18-20), which explains why the move of the Holy Spirit today (sometimes called the Charismatic or Renewal movement) has been so strongly opposed by every stream of religious tradition within the universal church.

Let us consider the facts for a moment. Even today after more than thirty years since the Charismatic movement spilled over into the historic church denominations and became the Renewal movement there still remains basic division and disunity between the two. "Opposition" would not be too strong a word to describe the traditional churches stand against the Renewal movement, and yet both claim to be led by and under the Lordship of the Holy Spirit.

Now if it is true that THE HOLY SPIRIT DOES NOT OPPOSE HIMSELF, and that the evil one and his powers of darkness are behind every opposition to the Holy Spirit, notwithstanding the fact that there will be some mixture of both truth and error on each side, **one of the parties has to be basically right and the other basically deceived!**

We are therefore left with two possible conclusions which need to be faced with courage and honesty:-

(i) *The historic churches are basically controlled by the Holy Spirit and the Renewal movement is basically inspired by demonic forces,*

OR

(ii) *The Renewal movement is basically inspired by the*

Holy Spirit and the historic churches are basically control-led by demonic forces.

How then do we arrive at the right answer? Well, taking the historical evidence first, let us consider who was on the Holy Spirit's side and who was on the evil one's side in the clashes between:

a)   the Church and the Reformers in the sixteenth century?
b)   the Church and the Wesleyan preachers of the eight-eenth century?
c)   the Church and the Pentecostals of the twentieth cen-tury?

Have you formed an opinion drawn from history?

Now let us consider the biblical evidence. Who was on the Holy Spirit's side and who was on the evil one's side in the clashes between:

a)   the Synagogues (Church) and the Lord Jesus?
b)   the Synagogues (Church) and the Apostles?

Clearly the Church (people) of God have resisted the Holy Spirit down through the Ages, as Stephen testi-fied (Acts 7:51).

One final question relating to church practice today. How is it that church leaders have no objection to the hiring of church halls for the purpose of yoga, transcendental medi-tation, martial arts and other demonic activities, but will forbid the use of such halls for the delivering of God's chil-dren from the powers of darkness? Who desires to PRE-VENT deliverance – the Holy Spirit or satan?? And how does satan exercise his control over the historic churches? The answer is – mainly through religious intellectuals.

Because of this unclean domination factor intellectuals have always and will always fight against the supernatural and revelational activities of the Holy Spirit. **The Bishop of Bristol** was once reputed to have said to **John Wesley,** *"Pretending to experiences of the Holy Spirit is a very horrid thing Mr. Wesley, a very horrid thing!"*

When the Most High, the Almighty, moves into our lives by the moving of His Holy Spirit, all that existed before is shaken and there is conflict, which produces either the leaven of the Pharisees or the fruit of the Spirit, and so often we are a mixture of both.

Of course, not all religious scholars are controlled by deep and hidden motives of pride, deceit, subtlety, ambition, unbelief and partyism? There are some like **Nicodemus,** to whom the Pharisees paid *no* attention (John 7:48-52), and **Gamaliel,** to whom the Pharisees paid *some* attention (Acts 5:33-40), and of course Saul who became Paul. Praise the Lord that the Sauls of this world have the potential in Christ to become Pauls! They are genuinely humble before God, as distinct from religious, and are able to use their great knowledge of the scriptures in their original languages so as to provide the people of God with accurate translations of the Word of God, and sound teaching from it. They know that *the letter kills but the Spirit gives life* **(2 Cor. 3:6)** and they use their knowledge, not as a master, but as a servant, allowing the Holy Spirit to use them for His revelational purposes.

The Holy Spirit must always have His personal say in our hearts and lives, no matter how clever, legal and "mathematical" we become, and the bottom line is being dead to self and alive to Christ so that we can be led by His Spirit. This is just as big a challenge, if not even bigger, for the scholars as for all of us who are Born Again.

Scholars are servants of the Lord like you and me and they can be as blind and as demonised as you and me, so do not be afraid of them.

Unfortunately the unpleasant truth which must be faced up to and prepared for by every sincere Christian today is that religious scholars, that is, the RULING MAJORITY, always, always, ALWAYS resist the Holy Spirit[1] (Acts 7:51). It usually takes a whole generation to pass by, in order for God's reforms to endure; for example the Reformation of the sixteenth century, the Wesleyan Revival of the eighteenth century and the Pentecostal Renewal of this twentieth century. The difference today is that I do not think we have a generation time span left in which to prepare for the huge restoration changes that God is purposing to do, and that is why I am writing so uncompromisingly, not to cause hurt, but to warn and protect the true Bride of Christ.

An historic church spokesman was reported[2] to have said that his Church took **a careful view** of (demon) *"possession"* and *"exorcism"* but it is quite apparent that these terms have never even been properly defined,[3] because if they had been defined in the normal way from the scriptures they would never be used by theologians and/or spokesmen at all, except to discount them.

Any trained minister who has done his basic homework would NEVER use the terms "demon-possession" or "exorcism" except to dismiss them from his Christian vocabulary. There is no such phrase as "demon-possession" in

---

[1] As Stephen was full of the Holy Spirit when he said this (Acts 7:55), it is plain that the Holy Spirit Himself is using Stephen to complain about resistance to Himself by religious people down through the ages.
[2] The Sun 4th June, 1986.
[3] See Book 1 Chapter 1 for definitions.

the Greek New Testament according to the best dictionaries, and "exorcism" is used only twice, and never as a description of the successful Christian ministry of casting out demons. Therefore any "careful view" that uses these terms when expressing a Christian standpoint has been superficial to say the least. One has to ask if this "careful view" is inspired by concern for:

(i)   The demonised sufferer?
(ii) Church tradition?
(iii) Avoiding battle with demonic forces?

We suspect the official answer would be (i) above but God looks on the heart (1 Sam. 16:7) and knows the whole truth, even though we may deceive ourselves.

Some apprehension at the prospect of casting out your first demon is both understandable and normal, but it is hard to see how a minister can be ordained or appointed as a shepherd over a flock of God's sheep without being able to defend or loose them from demonic forces.

However, what is totally indefensible is seeking to defend one's traditions against a salvation ministry which has been obtained by the blood of Christ Jesus and commanded in the Word of God (Mark 7:5-9, 13). That kind of "careful view" we can all do without.

In a newspaper article (Sun-Herald 30th July 1986) different church denominational spokesmen were alleged to have said:

> "(I have) never seen any real demon possessions in 27 years in the psychiatric field."
> "There are a growing number of 'quasi' possessions where people think they are possessed but it is really

*due to anxiety, psychological troubles, depression
and the power of suggestion,"*
R.C. Psychiatric Hospital Chaplain

*"....it is not the commission of the Christian Church to
engage in exorcisms."*
*"it's not commanded to be done and we do not have
the ability to do it," he said.*
*"We don't have the ability of Jesus Christ to cast out
demons. We believe it was a gift given exclusively to
the apostles and that it passed away with the apostles.*
Jehovah Witness spokesman

*"There is little in the New Testament to suggest that
exorcism was or should be a continuing practice by
Christians....*
*"There is little evidence that it was practised in the first
200 years of the early church and little evidence that it
should be encouraged in the church today.*
*"I think people too quickly attribute things such as sick-
ness and personal problems to the work of Satan. They
need doctors or psychiatrists or prayer before they
need exorcism."*
Protestant spokesman

Such is the quality of advice given by a range of traditional
church spokesmen!

Now you can see why I said that you have no need to be
afraid of Religious Scholars. One spokesman, surrounded
by demonised people for 27 years, says he has seen nothing, admitting his blindness. Another, having learnt from
the sons of Sceva, admits that the deliverance ministry is
beyond their membership's ability, thereby further admitting by implication that the same Spirit which raised Christ
from the dead does not dwell in them, and their religion is

inspired by a different spirit (2 Cor. 11:4). And yet another dismisses the **Great Commission** of our Lord Jesus Christ, with its claim of authority over all the powers of darkness (Luke 10:19, Matt. 10:1, 28:18-20), given to EVERY disciple to the close of the Age, as "little evidence". Thank God for the Pentecostals!

Are we not commanded to teach new disciples to KEEP STRICTLY, PRESERVE, GUARD, OBSERVE EVERYTHING THE Lord has **commanded** those early disciples TO THE CLOSE OF THE AGE? You can call that "little evidence" if you choose but I call it an ORDER! There is as much, if not more evidence in the New Testament for deliverance than there is for either water baptism or Holy Communion!

Obviously men can only say what they see and think to be right: if they have no discernment—if they do not perceive the true spiritual situation—if they do not see the spiritual battle - lines which have been drawn one cannot condemn, one can only pray, as did **Elisha** for his assistant *"Lord, open his eyes that he may see"* (2 Kings 6:17). And the Lord did, and the young man saw that although the armies of flesh outnumbered them, the "invisible" army of the Lord was greater still.

This is no light matter. The blindness of Christian leaders is holding up the preparation of the Bride of Christ. *The Bride will not make herself ready in the way that Christ desires her to - inner cleansing - **until she sees that she needs to do so,*** and she will not see that need while she is led by blinded leaders who unwittingly do satan's work for him. We who are into, or coming into, deliverance work need to pray like Elisha and like the Reformer and translator **William Tyndale** who was called "the father of the English Bible", and who, about to be burnt at the stake, prayed *"Lord, open the King of England's eyes!"* (1536 A.D.).

Most Christians know the story of the highly trained Phari-see named **Saul** whose zeal for God was so great that he busied himself travelling the country and searching out Christians whom he could accuse of blasphemy against God and orchestrate their execution (Acts 8:1-3, 9:1-2). How many Christians Saul was responsible for executing we do not know. One could roughly liken it to the regular execution of Christian pastors and their families in the 1980s by communist guerillas in the Philippines for preaching truths unsympathetic to the Communist cause. But such blood is not spilt in vain. Except a seed fall to the ground and die it cannot bear much fruit (John 12:24), and eventu-ally the blood and sacrifice of Christian Filipinos will bear a great harvest for the Kingdom of God in their nation.

And so it was with Saul. The comparatively few lives he took when fighting against the truth of Christ, brought forth a great harvest after his conversion. But before he could be used by the Lord in founding churches through many countries he had to be dealt with personally - a sort of "dying to self" and being raised to "newness of life" (Rom. 6:4). It was no accident that the religious scholar Saul was blinded on the road to Damascus and had to be led about by the hand for a season. He had been blind spiritually and then blinded physically so that he could understand his blindness and repent (change the direction of his life). He had to be shown how dark was the darkness in which he operated against the true people of God. And when the Lord gave him sight through the ministry of **Ananias** he received both physical *and* spiritual sight (Acts 9:1-22).

His experience enabled Saul, now **Paul,** to understand the blindness of others, for where they were, spiritually blind, he had once been himself (Acts 26:18). This experience enabled him to show **Elymas the Sorcerer** the blackness of his ways, not to utterly destroy the man but to bring him to repentance also, that his spirit might be saved in the Day of the Lord, even as the fornicator in the Church at Corinth had been dealt with (Acts 13:9-12, 1 Cor. 5:5).

It is the Lord who opens blind eyes, through the ministry of His Word! (Acts 26:16-18, 2 Cor. 3:14-4:6). May the good Lord and Father of us all, open OUR eyes to all His majestic purposes, that we shall be helps and not hindrances to His unfolding will, in Jesus' Name! Amen!

A more accurate viewpoint than the churchmen quoted is taken by **Professor Peter Wagner** of **Fuller Theological Seminary,** Pasadena, California. **"Restore Magazine"** (March '85) quoted him as saying:

"I think that we haven't even begun to tap the resources that we have in the ministries of deliverance. I think we haven't begun to recognize the actual direct power of evil in our lives. I am beginning to wonder if we've been playing games, particularly talking about Christian social action or political action or overthrowing governments. The way I am beginning to see it is that these kind of approaches may be trivial because we battle against the principalities and powers, and those aren't the presidents and dictators of the world; those are the demonic forces. If we don't learn how to confront these demonic forces directly in a spiritual battle, I think WE ARE PLAYING GAMES."

Persecuted Pastors and Christians everywhere - confront your *real* enemies! If it can be said that the Pentecostals and the Renewal or Charismatic Churches have been "playing games" by ministering a little bit of deliverance here and there when absolutely necessary - if **they** are to be described as being on the playing field and at least ready for **some** action – what can we say of the traditional churches? I speak this way not to be unkind but in the prayerful hope that SOMEONE in traditional leadership SOME-WHERE, will WAKE UP out of (spiritual) sleep! The night is far gone, the DAY is at hand! (Romans 13:11-12).

But someone will say that we are not supposed to include Jesus' earlier instructions for the training missions of the **twelve** and the **seventy** disciples and bring them under the authority of the Great Commission. They will point to the fact that those early missions included orders not to take gold, silver, copper, bag, sandals, staff, and only one coat (tunic) which orders are not applied today, and ignore the fact that *these* instructions (Matt. 10:9-10, Luke 9:3) were **later retracted by the Lord** (Luke 22:35-38) and therefore are clearly not automatically binding on future disciples.

Likewise the command not to go to the Gentiles or Samaritans is also plainly obsolete (Matt. 10:5-6) because the Lord reversed that with his vision to Peter (Acts 10:9-17) which led to the *Gentile* Pentecost (Acts 10:44-48).

So we can see that SOME commands to do with the training of the original disciples are later reversed by the Lord, but WHERE is the command NOT to preach, NOT to HEAL the sick? NOT to RAISE the dead, NOT to CLEANSE lepers and NOT to CAST OUT demons? (Matt. 10:1, 7-8).

In 1971 a conference was held in Sydney to debate the challenge of the then "Charismatic Movement" to normal evangelical Christianity. The conference was held at an inner city church which acted as "home" church to many Sydney University students and when the conference began the church hall was full of students, lecturers and clergy.

However, within a few minutes the speakers from both sides of the debate had resorted to a close examination of the

Greek New Testament and the vast majority of those attending were lost in a maze of Greek grammar which was
well "over their heads". Notwithstanding the confusion, this
involvement of the Greek language was essential for legiti-
mate theological debate and could not be avoided.

Obviously being able to translate from the original languages is a very great help to the genuine Bible student
because within the accurate translation of the scripture text
lies the truth of God's mind and therefore many points of
debate are best argued from the original languages where
possible.

On the other hand, some Bible scholars (I should really
call them Bible students in order not to minister to their
pride) may take a Bible discussion into the Hebrew or Greek
grammar, not for the purposes of obtaining a true understanding but in order to avoid defeat at the hands of a
more perceptive but insufficiently trained brother or sister.
By taking a discussion into territory where the layman cannot pursue his or her argument effectively the lay person is
disadvantaged so that they can seldom win their point,
and conversely, the scholar can seldom lose. The lay person
gets confused and the scholar saves face - not a very good
result for the Body of Christ whichever way you look at it!

Most Bible students who have been trained in a biblical
language would admit (with an inner smile) to having been
tempted successfully in this matter. And most would probably also admit, upon reflection, that such motivation is
really quite sneaky – or should I say snakey!

Such conduct is a classic example of handling the Word of
God deceitfully (2 Cor. 4:2).

The good news is that there is absolutely no escape or
refuge for the traditional Bible student when turning to the

inspired Greek[1] New Testament in order to escape the truth of, and the need for the deliverance ministry today. The language there is even more explicit and emphatic than the translated English text – Praise the Lord (e.g. Matt. 10:1 with 28:20).

We also have to face the fact that some Christian leaders do not always believe all of the Bible. Do not be afraid of them. You will remember[2] that the Lord Himself calls them blind guides whose words will not help you.

I went to one major theological college for a panel on the subject of "exorcism" some time ago and the reaction from the lecturing staff was nothing short of amazing. They had great difficulty in accepting that the Bible might be true in this field and had held the view for some time that the Bible was written in terms that peasants could understand but we, of course, are so clever now that we don't need to worry about that kind of terminology, we need to update it to a scientific age and consequently we have to de-my-thologise the Bible in order to present it to this modern age. Praise God, Christ through his mighty Spirit is destroying that kind of thinking today.

I believe that men who think in that way and who are sincere in their love of God will be agonising about this topic and they are going to have to change their theology. That is not easy. If you have built up a systematic theology it may be very, very difficult to accept God's correction through other men and that is something with which nearly all of us have to wrestle, if we are to continue growing as Christians.

[1] Some scholars have turned to Aramaic and Latin translations in order to support their theories, but the fact remains that it is the Greek text ALONE which is universally recognised as being inspired (written) by the Holy Spirit and has therefore been considered theologically infallible from apostolic times.
[2] Chap. 8.1 (ii)

A Serious Error

Following on the misunderstanding of the ministry by Jesus' friends and relatives, the gospel of Mark goes on to tell us of the charge laid fairly regularly by the scribes against Jesus, of ministering by **Beelzebub[1]**, a derogatory term for satan or a demon prince.

> **"And when his friends heard it, they went out to seize him, for they said, 'He is beside himself'. And the scribes who came down from Jerusalem said, 'He has Beelzebub, and by the prince of demons he casts out the demons.'" (Mark 3:21-22 -see also Matt. 12:24, 9:34, Luke 11:15).**

One can readily understand the serious nature of this charge. Yes, a mighty miracle had been done and yes, the ministry was successful, but who has inspired it - God or the devil? A fair question to ask oneself about any supernatural activity but it is the answer that will either justify or condemn, and so great care is needed. The scribes think they know the answer. They have been sent all the way from Jerusalem to Capernaum to put Jesus' ministry under their spiritual microscope. They are obviously "great ones" who would be able to put down the rabbi Jesus and tear his theology apart should it contain any flaw or weakness, and thus stop the rot in the early stages. The prejudice built up through earlier reports of his miracles and teaching no doubt was quickly inflamed within them when they were present during Jesus' ministry. Because their theology was of such rigid interpretation the only possible answer open to them was that Christ's power came from the prince of demons. A most serious charge and far too loosely thrown about, even today. Great care is needed before one makes accusations and charges as serious as this.

---

[1]Aramaic: "Lord of the dwelling;" Hebrew "Lord of dung." See also 2 Kings 1:2.

This kind of charge, when it is laid today, is usually made by implication, such implication being made by quoting:

> *"On that day many will say to me, 'Lord, Lord, did we not **prophesy** in your name, and **cast out demons** in your name, and do many **mighty works** in your name?***
>
> *And then will I declare to them, 'I never knew you; depart from me, you evildoers.'"* (Matt. 7:22-23)

These words of the Lord obviously bring a note of caution and there are four (4) basic KEYS to the right understanding of the passage:

(a) This teaching is directed against NON-CHRISTIAN ministers and ministries, those with whom the Lord does NOT have a personal relationship. It is NOT directed against **prophets, deliverance ministers** and **miracle workers** KNOWN BY THE LORD but against those whom He does NOT know, even though they may use His Name as did the seven sons of Sceva (Acts 19:15).

Here the Lord is exposing the existence of unregenerate ministers using counterfeit gifts, who, although they use the Name of Jesus, have not been BORN AGAIN, do not have the POWER of the Holy Spirit and have not been CALLED to minister by Him. Jesus plainly says of these ministers that He NEVER knew them (at any time) i.e. they have never had the seal, the earnest, the guarantee of His Spirit indwelling them (Rom. 8:9B, 2 Cor. 1:21-22, Eph. 1:13-14). No soundly converted and instructed Christian need fear that this passage is directed AT them, but rather FOR their protection against the counterfeits.

(b) The proof of the genuineness of a Christian ministry

is not the exercise of the gifts of the Spirit, but **the FRUIT of the Spirit** (Mark 4:8-9, 20; John 14:21-15:17; Gal. 5:22-23; Col. 3:12-15).

Here I must share with you some very important lessons learned through a gifted Christian minister losing her direction, in spite of her wonderful anointing (calling).

A Good Ministry

I was only two years in deliverance ministry when a lady joined the team I was leading and quickly established herself as the most talented and gifted deliverance minister of us all. It seemed that no enemy spirit could stand against her. Working closely with her was another Christian lady who brought prophecies and words of knowledge to guide her - and me - from time to time.

Misgivings

However some of the leadings did not sit too well in my spirit and I began to find myself being led in a direction that made me uncomfortable. They also exalted the lady minister. The sufferers "adored" her and because she was so effective and apparently directed by the Lord, Verlie and I 'flowed" as best we could.

Things soon reached the stage where she took control of the ministry as Director and senior minister, with myself only a figurehead. Two male full-time co-workers obeyed her every wish and whenever I questioned the direction or actions taken, the other three backed her up, against me. Verlie and I prayed fervently[1] for six months for the Lord to remove us (by grace) from the work before she told me we had to go. Our sacking was just about the only way we

---

[1] We did not really know what fervent prayer was, until then!

could be sure the Lord had heard our prayers and released us with His favour. That was probably our finest day during 1978, praise the Lord!

Vindication!

Now in February 1997, nearly twenty years later, the younger of the two male co-workers visited us to apologise and ask our forgiveness. He explained that the ministry had continued into all the characteristics of a cult or sect with everyone involved being fed lies and error, and afraid of offending the anointed one for fear of the wrath of God.

Post - Mortem

She had died in 1991 and now the two male leaders were busy still trying to heal the wounds and scars, and make restitution to all the damaged supporters, where appropriate.

What went wrong? The brother who visited me believes that three factors were vital in achieving all the deception:

(i)   **effective casting out of demons in Jesus Name**
(ii) **guidance primarily by prophecies, which became more and more of a deceptive mixture**
(iii) **genuine fear of the Lord**

and I would add:

(iv) **the occasional mighty work to keep the membership impressed**
(v)   **authoritative and total control by a woman[1] who was not herself under the authority of a man and therefore unprotected from powerful spiritual**

---

[1] See our book **"Headcovering and Lady Pastor-Teachers"**

forces (1 Cor. 11:1-16, 1 Tim. 2:8-15). This, I believe, is where the wheels fell off.

Male leaders were supposed to be her spiritual covering but in fact they did what she wanted, because she was "the Lord's Anointed" (cf. false christs, anointeds - Matt. 24:23-24).

I was the only dissenting voice, especially with the rigid controls being increasingly applied.

You will notice the deception carried all three of the ministries that the Lord Jesus warned us against – **prophecy, casting out demons and mighty works,** the only difference is that this work began as a **genuine** ministry and mixed prophecies led it astray, whereas the Lord referred specifically to ministries that were NEVER genuine, that is, carried out by people He NEVER KNEW!

Control Through Prophecies. How it was done!

A further note on the mixed and false prophecies. When the lady deliverance minister and I would disagree on a course of action it was her practice to tell the team that she would get a word from the Lord through the lady prophetess (her maidservant). To my regular consternation the prophecies that came forth ALWAYS supported my "opponent". When I asked my apologiser for his explanation how this could happen he commented that she often discussed her ideas with the prophetess (they were very close at that time) **before** seeking the prophecy. In other words she sowed her thoughts into the spirit of the prophetess who was dedicated to her, and thus obtained the authority she needed, apparently from the Throne of God. No one stood a chance against such subtlety, because there was always enough truth in the mix to sound convincing, and no one was going to oppose the Lord!

Fruit ???

Before she died the senior minister's behaviour began to deteriorate, becoming more and more controlling, difficult and demanding. As the co-worker said, there was little, if any, fruit of the Spirit. Even today I can hardly believe that what began as a powerful, anointed Christian ministry could become such a disaster, hurting so many lives. **Truly it is the FRUIT that testifies to the genuineness of a ministry!**

(c) This fruit is to be manifested by the MINISTERS, i.e., the shepherds, not necessarily the sheep. Obviously it is the ministers who minister **prophecy, deliverance** and **miracle** ministries, so when we are discerning a work or ministry of God we should look at the MINISTERS. We cannot always judge a work by the condition of the sheep because *a genuine work of God will always attract the most spiritually bound up and needy people.* If you ONLY have "beautiful" people in your flock that will certainly impress man but it may not impress the Lord!

Another Error

A Christian brother once challenged me about the spiritual condition of a precious sister who had been receiving deliverance for some time. Apparently he had come across her when she had been manifesting uncleanness from her mouth and had thought "If that is the way a Christian speaks after going regularly to the Hobson's deliverance meeting then their ministry is suspect because we know things by their fruit".

The Reality

On the face of it that seems like a fair comment but in fact it is seriously astray because of lack of information. In the first place it does not take into account the amount of

_n that dwells in an "ordinary" Christian. It is not re-
alistic to think that 200 years of pollution (at least four
generations of hereditary problems, plus what we have
added in our own generation and life-time) can be removed
in 6 months. Secondly it does not take into account that
deliverance ministry has caused many unclean spirits to
surface in the human personality, so that a sufferer's personality can be quite a mixture during the course of a day.
There may be times when the Christian in battle will lapse
in either speech or conduct as releases take place - usually nothing very serious. Better to lapse because of out-
going junk rather than incoming junk! And better still if
Christians experiencing deliverance were to be on their
guard and *"give no place to the devil"*, (Eph. 4:27) at all but
ensured that the praise of God was on their lips instead.

Please remember that deliverance ministers exercise their
ministry to many people who have tried everything else
available in the normal local church scene and who have
been put in their own pastor's "too hard file". They get ALL
the tough as well as some easy cases, humanly speaking,
by the grace of the Lord. To judge the spiritual condition of
a person receiving regular deliverance by one conversation is unrealistic. Also one has to take into account the
sufferer's *original* condition. If a sufferer is using unkind
language NOW whereas BEFORE they were using pro-
fane AND unkind language most of us would say there has
been some improvement.

So now we can see why the Lord tells us to judge a ministry BY THE FRUIT OF THE MINISTERS.

**(d) The Deliverance ministry is not reduced in value by
this passage but ELEVATED.** The passage clearly indicates that we will be able to discern the Lord's MINISTERS
from charlatans and counterfeiters *by their fruits rather than
their gifts;* but far from denigrating or demoting the ministry

of deliverance, as many tend to see it, this passage actu
ally elevates it.

To illustrate and underline His emphasis on the kind of fruit
that a real Christian Minister should bring forth in his or her
life, Jesus compares good fruit against THREE *MAJOR
AND IMPRESSIVE SUPERNATURAL ACTIVITIES.* He is
saying that EVEN IF you can do mighty works (i.e. as-
tounding miracles), EVEN IF you prophesy (a very highly
rated gift that we are to desire earnestly) and EVEN IF you
cast out demons (really striking at the Kingdom of satan),
but the FRUIT of the Holy Spirit and obedience to the
WORD and WILL of God is absent from your life, then in
reality you are working iniquity (drawing glory to yourself)
and the Lord doesn't know you and doesn't want to know
you. You are counterfeit! You can be "tops" in the spiritual
realm of gifts (and deliverance is a "top" gift) but it doesn't
mean a thing without "good fruit".

Manifesting fruit is manifesting the Lord who is IN you, and
working THROUGH you and therefore KNOWS you!

The scribes reaction then, was of slanderous and destructive character. They are indeed of their father the devil,
who is the father of lies (John 8:44), as Jesus said. I can
remember a young man in my parish in the early part of
this ministry coming to me (before the takeover) and saying. "How do you know that what you are doing is not
satanic? How do you know that you are casting out demons by the power of God and not from satanic power?"
Now that's a reasonable question, even though the spirit
behind the question was not of the Lord, and I did my best
to answer it. It's the sort of question that would crop up in
anybody's mind who has not examined this area of the
New Testament. I think it is helpful to be challenged afresh
because it makes you look at your ministry again. It makes
you ask the Lord yet again, "Now, Lord, what am I doing?

Am I really doing this in your Name? Or have I got into some kind of occult deception that I don't know anything about?" I was musing on such things one day in the Church Hall kitchen at **St. Michaels, Flinders St., Sydney,** thinking about the mind-blowing days when the ministry began and wondering where it was all going to lead, when my eyes were suddenly rivetted on an old youth club banner propped against the wall. On the banner was a text which for some unearthly reason stood out like a beacon - "HOLD FAST THAT WHICH IS GOOD!" (1 Thess. 5:21)

Just before this I had been running through my check list again, perhaps for the hundredth time:-

1.   In whose **Name** was the ministry performed?

2.   By whose **authority** (Word) was the ministry performed?

3.   For whose **glory** was the ministry performed?

4.   By whose **Spirit** (power) was the ministry performed?

I really shouldn't have needed the rhema (personal, alive Word) from God, but with so many challenges flying around from supposedly biblical sources it was nice to have direct confirmation from the Lord Himself.

Thank God we have been enabled to hold fast that which is good through all the years of controversy, rejection and battle. Praise His Holy Name for the vindication of our calling.

So then, it is helpful to be challenged and to challenge oneself, but note Christ's reply to the Jewish leaders charge of "Beelzebub":

Jesus's response to Religious Scholars

(a)   "Knowing their thoughts, he said to them,

'Every kingdom divided against itself is laid waste, and no city or house divided against itself will stand; and if satan casts out satan, he is divided against himself; how then will his kingdom stand? And if I cast out demons by beelzebub, by whom do your sons cast them out? Therefore they shall be your judges. But if it is by the Spirit of God that I cast out demons, then the Kingdom of God has come upon you'." **(Matt. 12:25-28 R.S.V.)**

The first thing we should note from the text is that satan has a kingdom. We know that he has his kingdom on earth in as much as *the whole world lies in (the power of) the evil one* (1 John 5:19) and it is this kingdom against which the church is prevailing. The gates of Hades are the gates of the kingdom of satan but the question arises as to WHERE is this kingdom? If we look at the Kingdom of God we normally understand **kingdom** to mean **'rule',** and the text indicates that when the Holy Spirit casts out demons the rule or kingdom of satan is removed and replaced to that degree by the rule or Kingdom of God IN HUMAN BEINGS. THE RULE OR KINGDOM OF SATAN THERE-FORE RESIDES IN EVERY HEART AND EVERY MIND WHERE CHRIST IS NOT FULLY LORD (Acts 5:3, 2 Cor. 4:4, Eph. 2:1-2). **Such an unclean kingdom reveals it-self by the works of the flesh** or by even more obvious demonic behaviour, as against the Kingdom of God which is revealed through the fruit of the Spirit (Gal. 5:19-24).

Jesus spoke the above words in the context of the dra-matic healing and deliverance of a blind and dumb demo-niac. Satan had expanded his kingdom or rule in the unfor-tunate person to include blindness and dumbness, but not for long. What a mighty Saviour and Lord we have!

Jesus' response begins very graciously by illustration that if satan casts out satan, he is divided against himself and

112

his kingdom cannot stand. He then raises the question that if indeed He casts out demons by Beelzebub, as they charge, then by whom do other Jewish itinerant exorcists cast them out? He argues that as His ministry is so obviously superior to that of Jewish exorcists, who failed more often than not in their attempts to release the demonised, clearly their ministry must also be of satan, if they are correct in their accusations. Jewish exorcists did not carry anything like the authority of Jesus' ministry. They were nothing like as effective. The results of Christ's ministry were there, before their very eyes! If they are the results of satan's work what does that indicate about the work of others? But if He had cast out demons by the Spirit or finger (Luke 11:20) of God then the Kingdom of God had come upon them - for where the Holy Spirit delivers or rescues a creature of God from a form of demonisation, then to that extent the salvation of God has been manifested and the rule of God has been imposed.

(b)   "Or how can one enter a strong (man)'s house and plunder his vessels, unless he first binds the strong? Then indeed he may plunder his house. He who is not with me is against me, and he who does not gather with me scatters" (Matt. 12:29-30).

I must repeat here some of the things I said in Book 1 - they are just so important! The teaching about the binding of the strong (man) is fairly clear, except to say that the word "man" is not specifically included in the Greek text. Jesus succeeded where others failed because he used AUTHORITY to bind and render ineffective the powers of darkness, whether **ruler** or **authority,** "man" or **male spirit** within the demonised person. But then comes the cutting edge of His reply to the scribes and Pharisees: **"He that is not with me is against me, and he that does not gather with**

me scatters!" Jesus' words are getting close to the bone now and He challenges them very fiercely at this point.

Jesus means *"Now be very sure about this; you say that I have been casting out demons because I am the prince of demons. If that is right then you are safe, but remember this, you are either with me or against me. You have to sort yourselves out; you people have to make up your minds where you stand but be VERY CAREFUL because if you are WRONG you are treading on VERY dangerous ground."*

The Christian cannot sit on the fence regarding Christ's deliverance ministry - it will sort you out - *HE* will sort you out and shake you like you have never been sorted out and shaken before. You say you are a Christian? You say you have fully committed your life to Christ whatever the cost? Then you dare not make a mistake about your assessment of a deliverance ministry! Because if it is Christ's, then the Kingdom of God is right there and you cannot even stand by neutrally. You must be committed to support that work of His Spirit at least morally, for IF YOU ARE NOT WITH HIM YOU ARE AGAINST HIM. Do you believe this? Let me say it again, IF YOU ARE NOT WITH HIM YOU ARE AGAINST HIM! It is the plain meaning of Jesus' words. All the verbiage about being a disciple, believing God's Word, being a son of the Reformation, an evangelical or a Pentecostal or a Catholic or this or that etc. IS JUST SO MUCH WORTHLESS HOT AIR unless you can stand with Christ in His deliverance work and say "I am with you Lord!" Amen? Hallelujah!

Being able to do this, Jesus says, qualifies YOU as a gatherer with Him and being unable to do this makes YOU a scatterer, that is, GATHERING FOR the Kingdom of God or SCATTERING FROM the Kingdom of God - a sheep, or a **wolf!** When the Lord warned us of wolves in sheep's clothing He surely meant to warn us not to be deceived by

114

the APPEARANCE of "Christians" but to observe whether or not they bore good fruit or taught destructive heresies (Matt. 7:15, 2 Peter 2:1-2).

> **(c)** **"Therefore I tell you, every sin and blasphemy will be forgiven men, but the blasphemy against the Spirit will not be forgiven. And whoever says a word against the Son of man will be forgiven; but whoever speaks against the Holy Spirit will not be forgiven, either in this age or in the age to come."**
>
> **(Matt. 12:31-32 R.S.V.)**

Now this is the most severe condemnation and rebuke, I think, in the whole of the New Testament, and it is levelled at the scribes and Pharisees who have accused the Lord of having the Prince of demons. There is no way in the world, in spite of commentators and preachers who think otherwise, you can wriggle this passage around and obtain the meaning that the unforgivable sin is the rejection of Christ. The passage simply does not say that. It is talking about blasphemy and speaking against the Holy Spirit. You can reject Christ in this life and be forgiven. Many of us rejected Christ for years before we were converted but it was forgiven us. That is a forgivable sin IN THIS LIFE for those who eventually repent and receive Him, but the blasphemy and the speaking against the Holy Spirit IS NOT FORGIVABLE IN THIS LIFE or in the life to come.

Here Jesus increases His judgment against His accusers with withering force. Some people have thought of this as only a warning rather than a judgment, but while it is bad enough for Christ's friends to think He is mentally unbalanced because He ministers deliverance, it is even worse for others who should know better, such as religious scholars of the Word of God. They expose themselves to the great danger of speaking against the Holy Spirit. Mark records that Jesus gives this reply because they had said *"He has an unclean spirit",* and therefore **in attacking a genuine ministry of the Spirit they are very close to speaking against the PERSON** of the Spirit. There is a serious lesson here for all of us (cf Mark 3:28-30), especially Christian leaders who have enough "head knowledge" to get themselves into serious trouble.

Summary

The main message of this section is NOT to be afraid or in awe of Religious Scholars. Respect them as you would any brother or sister for whom Christ died. Love them, but don't be controlled by them (your Pastor excluded, in some circumstances). If I had been in awe of or afraid of Religious Scholars, or even followed their advice twenty two years ago, we (Verlie and I) would not have the anointing we now have on our lives, neither would these books have been written to advance the cause of Christ's Full Salvation for mankind. I am not, of course, advocating disobedience of church leaders but OBEDIENCE TO THE HOLY SPIRIT! (Acts 4:18-20, 5:29)

And now a word to Pastors, scholars and leaders.

I ask you to consider for a moment the Word of the Lord in the tenth chapter of John's gospel. Jesus said:

> **"I am the good shepherd: the good shepherd lays down His life for the sheep."**
> **"He who is a hireling and not a shepherd, who is not the owner of the sheep, beholds the wolf coming, and leaves the sheep, and flees, and the wolf snatches them, and scatters them."**
> **"He flees because he is a hireling, and is not concerned about the sheep." (John 10:11-13).**

The warning is clear. There are **genuine shepherds** under

the lordship of the good Shepherd, and there are **hirelings** who put their own safety first. Let each one of us who are shepherds take heed to be found faithful in the face of the wolves.

Let us also remember the Lord's warning to the scholars of His day **"The first shall be last and the last first"** (Matt. 19:30, 20:16; Luke 13:30, Mark 10:31). We live at a time when Jesus' words will be amply demonstrated. Let us not oppose His Word or His Holy Spirit, lest we be found to be enemies of God, and having begun the race well, run last.

I conclude this section on the dangers of **unclean spirits of intellectualism** in the Church with quotes from a prophetic word, and a Word from Jesus in the New Testament:

PROPHECY, DELIVERANCE and RESTORATION MEETING - 22nd November, 1987

First Prophet:

"THUS SAITH THE LORD:

... AS I SHAKE NOT ONLY THE HEAVENS AND THE EARTH, BUT IN PARTICULAR SHAKE THE NATIONS AND MY CHURCH, I WOULD WISH YOU TO UNDERSTAND THAT THE FIRST SHALL, ON MANY OCCASIONS, BECOME LAST. AND I WOULD HAVE YOU UNDERSTAND THAT THOSE WHOM EVEN MY CHILDREN WOULD SEE AS LAST - LAST IN IMPORTANCE, LAST IN EFFICIENCY, LAST IN ABILITY, LAST IN POTENTIAL TO FULFIL MY PURPOSES - IT IS WITH THESE VERY CHOSEN ONES THAT I WILL SHOW FORTH MY POWER; I WILL SHOW FORTH MY ABILITY TO CHANGE LIVES. I WILL GET MYSELF GLORY NOT ONLY FROM THE WEAK AND THE FOOLISH THINGS OF THE EARTH, BUT FROM THOSE WHO ARE COUNTED LAST.

SO I WARN YOU TODAY MY CHILDREN: DO NOT BE SURPRISED AT THE THINGS THAT COME TO PASS. DO NOT BE SURPRISED AT THOSE WHOM I CHOOSE TO SERVE ME IN THIS WAY OR THAT, FOR I WILL CHOOSE THOSE WHOM YOU WOULD NOT,

AND I WILL CHOOSE THESE CHOSEN TO SHOW FORTH MY GLORY AND MY POWER. DO NOT THEREFORE BE SURPRISED OR CONFOUNDED OR CONFUSED, FOR I WILL BY-PASS THE GREAT AND MIGHTY AND WILL CHOOSE WHOM I WISH.

THEREFORE, EACH AND EVERY ONE OF YOU IF YOU WOULD SERVE ME, BECOME SERVANTS. TAKE NO ACCOUNT OF THE OPINIONS OF MEN OR OF THEIR VALUATIONS. DO NOT SAY TO YOURSELVES, "I AM WORTHLESS", BUT SAY TO YOUR-SELF, "I AM A CHILD OF GOD AND, ALTHOUGH I AM OF NO ACCOUNT IN THE EYES OF MEN, YET WILL THE LORD USE ME, AND I WILL BE HIS INSTRUMENT FOR HIS GLORY...

Second Prophet continuing

"I SAY TO YOU THIS DAY TO SEEK MY FACE IN A MANNER THAT YOU HAVE NEVER DONE BEFORE. I SAY AGAIN MY CHIL-DREN TO YOU THIS DAY: SEEK MY FACE IN A MANNER THAT YOU HAVE NEVER SOUGHT ME BEFORE. FOR IN THESE DAYS THAT ARE COMING UPON MY CHURCH, I WILL BE FOUND OF THEM ONLY WHO SEEK DILIGENTLY TO SEE MY FACE AND TO SEEK MY WAYS AND TO WALK IN MY PATHS.

BE INSTRUCTED BY ME, BECAUSE IN THESE LAST DAYS THERE WILL BE MANY FALSE SPIRITS, BUT ONLY ONE HOLY SPIRIT. SO SEEK MY FACE AND BE TAUGHT AND LED BY MY **HOLY** SPIRIT AND YOU SHALL NOT FALL. THOUGH THE FALL-ING WILL BE GREAT FOR MANY, YOU MY CHILDREN WHO SEEK MY FACE WILL STAND AND YOU SHALL SEE THE DAY OF THE LORD...."

And, as the Lord Jesus has taught ALL of us: **"BEWARE OF THE LEAVEN OF THE PHARISEES"**

(d) Other Deliverance Ministers

(i) **"John said to him (Jesus) 'Teacher, we saw someone casting out demons in your Name WHO DOES NOT FOLLOW US, and we for-bade him, BECAUSE HE WAS NOT FOLLOW-ING US.' But Jesus said, 'Do not forbid him,**

> **for there is no one who shall do a mighty work
> on (in) my Name and will be able quickly to
> speak evil of me, for he who is not against us,
> is for us.'"**

> **(Mark 9:38-40 Lit.)**

Perhaps it ought not to surprise us but it seems a little
strange to many people that **even deliverance ministers**
may also oppose the ministry of deliverance - **when it is
carried out by others;** situations can arise where it is not
so much WHAT you do but the WAY that you do it, as well
as the REASON WHY and by WHOSE authority, that raises
questions.

The above passage puts some very powerful and perti-
nent questions to us today (e.g. compare the sons of Sceva)
but I wish to confine myself here to two points - THE REA-
SON WHY the disciples forbade the ministry by an unknown, which is plainly given as *"BECAUSE he was not
following us"* - and their correction by the Lord Jesus.

The fact of the matter is that when the Lord pours out His
Spirit in ANY age the movement of the Spirit flows freely
for a season and then becomes hindered as MEN begin to
organise themselves to accommodate the influx of converts.

Local churches and then church denominations are
founded, Constitutions and Articles of Religion are drawn
up, and MEN, good Christian men, begin to build up legalistic, theological walls between different expressions of the
Christian faith.

Obviously there are enormous advantages for people of
like mind associating themselves in the same expression
of faith and this enables them to keep the unity of the faith
that they share together in the bond of peace.

However, notwithstanding all the many advantages, the fact remains that Christian denominations and their Godly men often demand adherence to rules and regulations which should NOT be laid upon the backs of other Godly people, i.e. those regulations which are certainly not prov- able from Holy Scripture; and the disciples of today are sometimes no wiser in this matter than those early disci- ples who walked with Jesus.

Some disciples today (often very close to the Lord) are always telling other disciples or potential disciples that they must do this or they must not do that, e.g. *"You cannot minister Holy Communion because you are not an ordained priest"*, or *"You cannot baptise your converts because you are not a deacon,* (but it is good that you led them to Christ)", or *"You cannot minister the Word because have not been 'ordained' by a denomination and had hands laid on you"* etc. etc.

The early Pentecostals were virtually forced to begin a new denomination as the Holy Spirit swept forward in revival power and they broke away from all this man-made legal- ism. They went forward, not in man's traditions but in the Power of God.

Even the Pentecostals themselves (having become a tra- ditional denomination) are now in danger of repeating this old error (it is so hard to learn from history) because today they now ask *"Whose covering are you under? What group/ denomination do you belong to?"* While their intentions may be excellent we need to remind ourselves that the Spirit blows where HE wills! He can raise up stones to cry out HOSANNA if the rest of the church be silent and it be the will of God; and if He wants to call ANY child of God to do a job He doesn't need the permission of the denominations or ANYBODY ELSE. God Himself provides the covering for His chosen ones, as He did for the prophets of old and the apostles of our own dispensation (Gal. 1:1).

In the text quoted the minister *"did not follow after"* the Lord and His disciples and so the disciples forbade him (to minister). He was not ordained, was not trained (with their group), had not had hands laid on him and was not under their covering (a nice word for "authority") so as far as their fleshy minds were concerned it was not right and they stopped the unknown from ministering. It seems that the plight of the sufferer did not matter and the courage of the unknown was of no consequence.

Jesus' Response

I am so glad the Lord set the disciples straight. In a few words He swept away all their legalistic religiosity of the flesh and brought them back again into the realm of spiritual understanding!

So there we have it. **Even deliverance ministers (and others very close to the Lord, too!) can oppose a genuine deliverance ministry of God.** How careful we have to be.

I would like to complete this section by now looking at a far more joyous and encouraging reaction by the disciples, in order to balance the record:

(ii) **The seventy returned with joy, saying, "Lord, even the demons are subject to us in your name!" And He said to them, "I saw satan fall like lightning from heaven. Behold, *I have given you authority to tread upon serpents and scorpions, and over all the power of the***

enemy; and nothing shall hurt you. Nevertheless do not rejoice in this, that *the spirits are
subject to you;* but rejoice that your names
are written in heaven."
       (Luke 10:17-20 R.S.V. - emphasis mine).

Surely this passage must be one that brings joy and thrill
to every Christian heart! What Christian heart is there that
has not leaped for joy to discover that Jesus' every word
can be relied upon. It is not "all pie in the sky" theory but
Jesus is real, Jesus cares and Jesus IS Lord, and when
He gives you a job to do, you can do it because you *can
do all things* (that He requires of you) *through Christ
who strengthens you.* (Phil. 4:13).

You always believed and knew His Word could be relied
upon but we never tire of seeing Him perform that which
He has promised to do, when we are obedient to His commands. Some people expect "exorcists" to be gloomy, tired,
worn out shells, but they *know neither the scriptures nor
the power of God* (Mark 12:24). Any spiritual work can be
tiring, even exhausting, but the privilege of successfully
ministering salvation to a corrupted creature is sufficient to
bring joy and refreshment to any Christian's heart, as those
early disciples experienced!

Jesus' Response

First, the Lord confirms the strength of His disciples position and secondly assures them of their personal safety.
You may remember that there is a triple negative in the
Greek text which gives enormous emphasis to His words
" - *NOT anything NOT NOT shall hurt you"* (v.19). Thirdly,
without deflating their joy, He cautions them to put things in
their proper perspective. There are TWO very good reasons to be joyful. First and foremost because their names

are written in Heaven (cf. Rev. 20:11-15, 21:27). And secondly - because even the demons are subject to them in Jesus' name. It is good to get things in right perspective and priority.

(e)   Summary

I believe, considering all the evidence, it is true to say that the Christian ministry of deliverance put both Christ and the apostles into a considerable amount of bother, and that is to be expected when satan finds his network of power and authority over God's creation in the world being assailed.

Satan's favourite weapon, of course, is the church. To use pagans against the crucified Jesus is not nearly as satisfying to him as using blood-bought Christians. It is the same principle, of course, as the chosen people of God harassing and executing their Messiah (John 1:11). The Romans would never have bothered with an itinerant Rabbi if they had not been goaded and stirred up by the political actions of the Jewish leaders. Perhaps now we can understand more clearly what it means to walk in Jesus' footsteps, to be truly crucified with Christ. It is a lonely way - nobody (much) will want you or want to know you after, or even before heavy persecution comes. There will be triumphant moments such as the entry into Jerusalem, but when all the false witnesses and lies are brought together and there is danger in being loyal to the Truth, friends may be conspicuous by their absence. (Mark 14:50)

The fact that deliverance is a miracle ministry and its evidence abounds to the goodness of Christ Jesus will not count for much with those whose hearts have been hardened. **The Lord Jesus on earth had the most dynamic ministry the world had ever seen, yet His critics and**

detractors were legion. They hardened their hearts and sought to destroy Him. The evidence of His ministry did not convince them but instead showed them up for what they were and who was really their father (John 8:44). A thousand years before Christ it was written:

> "I am the Lord your God, who brought you up out of the land of Egypt.
>
> Open your mouth wide, and I will fill it. *But my people did not listen to my voice. Israel would have none of me.*
>
> So I gave them over to their stubborn hearts, to follow their own counsels. O that my people would listen to me, that Israel would walk in my ways!
>
> I would soon subdue their enemies, and turn my hand against their foes. Those who hate the Lord would cringe toward him, and their fate would last for ever.
>
> I would feed YOU with the finest of the wheat, and with honey from the rock I would satisfy you."
>
>   (Ps. 81:10-16. R.S.V. - emphasis mine).

Do not be deceived into thinking that this sinful generation is any different. It is just as well that the all-availing blood of Jesus covers and atones for all our sins or none of us could enter the Kingdom of Heaven.

We close this section with a reaction from the **Gerasene** people after the mighty deliverance of the man with the **Legion,** one of the saddest sentences in the Bible:

> "And those who had seen it told what had happened to the demonised man and to the swine. And *they began to beg Jesus to depart* from their neighbourhood."
>
>   **(Mark 5:16-17)**

Imagine it! A violent madman - one who could not be controlled or contained and who had been terrorising the neighbourhood is delivered in one afternoon, and instead of rejoicing and praising God, THEY COULD NOT WAIT TO GET RID OF JESUS. It was not the monetary loss of the swine that upset them primarily, because Luke's Gospel tells us that *"they were seized with great fear"* (Luke 8:37).

Even the disciple Peter experienced a similar desire to get rid of Jesus, or to put it more acceptably, the one who recognised he was sinful (full of sin?) wanted to distance himself from the Holy One and begged Jesus to leave:

"Depart from me for I am a sinful man, O Lord"
(Luke 5:8).

Perhaps his fear, confusion and sense of unworthiness was similar to that of the Gerasenes, and both these incidents bear thinking about for a moment. In the light of all that these books have been saying, e.g. the widespread nature of demonisation (and its relationship to sin, the spiritual disease of the human heart) and how this consists of kingdoms of the powers of darkness[1] is it any wonder that, seeing the man who had the Legion was freed, all the unclean kingdoms and their ruling spirits were at panic stations **within the souls of the Gerasenes?**

Why, at any moment Jesus might have turned on THEIR kingdoms and cast them out! They were not to know that He was confining Himself to OBVIOUS AND OUTWARD manifestations only, at that time in history, and that the FULL salvation of God in all its deep, cleansing and searching

---

[1] More fully explained in Book 4 or briefly in **"The Reincarnation Deception"** and **"End Time Deliverance and the Holy Spirit Rivival"**.

power was to be revealed in the End-Time some nineteen centuries later (1 Peter 1:5).

Let us reflect on this even further. Are the people with whom you have to do each day any different from the Gerasenes? We would like to think so, but let us be prepared. Jesus warned us that if they hated Him they would also hate those who follow Him. They are certainly going to fear those equipped with a measure of His power.

At the very least we can expect many people, even people who call themselves Christians to, like Peter, **distance themselves from exposure to the truth** and from Him who is the Truth. Jesus said that many that are first will be last, and the last first (Mark 10:31) and so we can expect many surprises as the Lord's "sorting out" gets under way.

However one thing that should NOT surprise deliverance ministers is an earnest request to depart from the assembly, parish or denomination to which they have belonged. **They are a threat to the hidden kingdoms and agencies of satan in EVERY place** (John 3:19-21).

Forewarned is forearmed.

CHAPTER 9

FAILURES

Let me say at the very beginning of this chapter that every faithful minister of the Lord will experience failure during the course of his or her ministry of healing and deliverance. I am bold enough to say that if you have never experienced failure in these areas you may belong to the group that takes a "careful view" to keep out of the action, except in the minor areas of warfare, such as against seasonal influenza or passing head-aches etc.

Any minister who goes forward with the Word of God into every crisis situation is going to fail sooner or later. Why? Because we begin as rank beginners who need considerable training, and that training is often accomplished in battle conditions. The cold, hard fact of the matter is that **we may learn ten times as much from a failure than from a victory,** or to put it another way, a failure will teach us as much as we can learn from ten victories. We discover that healing faith is not simply "easy believism", that more than pious or religious talk is necessary (1 Cor. 4:20), that we don't have as much power as we would like (Rev. 3:8), and when a failure drives us back into the Word of God for some answers, we discover that we don't know the Word of God as well as we thought we did.

I speak from sobering experience. As a young Curate back in 1971 I was posted to an evangelical church where, during a Parish Council meeting the young Council secretary was taken ill and assisted home. He was found to be riddled with terminal cancer throughout his body, and most of the church began to pray for strength for him in death, and strength for his young wife, and for the children.

However as a "convert" to the Holy Spirit Renewal movement I found some similar souls in the Parish and asked them to a special prayer meeting in order to lay hands on me for the express purpose of taking the healing power of Jesus to the hospital bed of young Jon (we shall call him). They prayed over me and commissioned me for the task and I went and ministered to Jon. The moment my hands touched his body he began to writhe in discomfort - not through pain but through the heat of the Holy Spirit supplied from the Throne of God. For forty minutes and through countless oooh's and aaah's he wriggled and squirmed under the fire in my hands, which had become the hands of the Lord.

However I began to get alarmed because I had instructions to join the Youth Fellowship at 5.00 pm which was my number one Parish priority and I knew what the senior minister expected of me. The fellowship was large, and full of university students who needed a fatherly eye kept on them. For me to be unreliable with the youth group was a serious enough matter, but for me to be late because I was ministering healing was totally unacceptable, because at that time the charismatic movement was a source of great embarrassment to conservative evangelical leaders, and opposed.

I stayed with Jon as long as I dared and left for the Youth Fellowship with mixed emotions. I was pleased that so much Holy Spirit heat had passed into Jon's body but I was also annoyed that my obligations to a religious system, combined with the unbelief of its leaders, had forced me to leave Jon while ministry heat was still flowing out of my hands.

To make a long story short Jon died some two or three months later than the doctors expected, and on the night he went to Glory I arrived at his home and looked into the eyes of his wife who asked me *"Why? What went wrong?"* I never want to face that question again from people who believed in the Lord, and who had come to believe in healing, and wanted it! I answered as best I could- "We are being taught - only learners at the moment - we will become so much more effective by God's grace in another ten years etc." all of which was true but of small comfort to that poor girl.

WHY DID I FAIL? I suppose I could blame the religious system where I had to squeeze a vital life-saving ministry in between other pressing Parish duties. Or I could blame the unbelief of the senior minister which forced me to act alone and without pastoral support. Or I could blame the vast majority of the Christians in that church who had accepted Jon's death as inevitable and were praying, believing that it was God's will for him to die.

But where would blaming one or more of those causes get me? How much better to look at myself and make sure that never again would I presume that enough power had been ministered into Jon over forty minutes. In future terminal cases, while the evidence of the heat of the Holy Spirit continued so I will CONTINUE to minister. Never again will I allow obedience to the traditions of men to put in jeopardy the life of another Christian. Never again will I underestimate the enemy and go into battle for a life without all guns (weapons, gifts) blazing. In future, by God's grace, it will be boots and all, to tread on the neck of the enemy (Josh. 10:24, Luke 10:19, Rom. 16:19-20).

Here is a prophetic word from the Lord received during our

130

Deliverance and Restoration meeting held 3rd August 1986:-

"THUS SAITH THE LORD

I am the Lord of Hosts. I am the Lord of Armies, and the victory which I have obtained for the children of God is indeed a mighty victory. It was obtained at great price, even the Blood of the only begotten Son of God. It is a victory which stands at the centre of history, and all things look towards it, and look back upon it as the time when I, El Shaddai, ordained the salvation of a people chosen by me, out of pollution and wickedness. This victory is yours.... ! It is a victory for the people of God everywhere, and not only shall no weapon that is formed against you prosper, not only shall the gates of Hades not prevail against you, but through this victory of my Son Jesus I have established that the people of God shall possess the earth... They shall have for their inheritance every good thing, and yet again I affirm to you, not one of my promises shall fail. You may know failure, as did my people entering the Promised Land, and as did the people I ordained to be redeemed and brought forth under the New Covenant, but you shall not be bound by it. Every failure that you experience shall be turned into a well of joy; you shall learn to overcome failure. You shall learn to overcome the enemy wherever he is to be found; you shall learn from your failures and move into continuous victory, for the Cross stands before you as an example of the victory which is yours.

Therefore, my children, do not be discouraged, do not let your hearts fail you for fear, but be strong in my Spirit, be strong in the knowledge that I am able, and

*indeed do strengthen you with might in the inner man....
where the Spirit of my Son dwells within you. My Spirit
witnesses to your spirit that the victory has been won,
and it only remains for you to move into its experience
in all its fulness.... This will not always be easy, but it is
yours for the taking.*

*Move forward in the Name and power of my Son, and
you shall know that what I have said to you this day (is
true, as it) becomes more and more real and true to
each one."*

9.1   FALSE FAILURES

Once we realise there will be genuine, but hopefully, temporary failures in any learning situation we ought also to
recognise there will be many FALSE failures, that is, ministry which appears to have achieved no visible benefit for
the sufferer but in fact there has been a spiritual or invisible change for the better of which the sufferer is unaware.

There are at least four (4) situations where **successful**
ministry may be thought of as having failed:

(i)   CONTINUATION OF BAD HABITS

Quite obviously the sufferer who continues to walk in the
lust of the flesh and the lust of the eyes and the pride of
life (1 John 2:16) will not hold or keep his or her deliverance very long and may even let spirits back into themselves worse than the originals. Such a person may claim
that the ministry or minister has failed but of course this
would be untrue. Demons were cast out but *responsibility
for their return* (in perhaps even greater strength) *must be
laid squarely on the sufferer, whether adequate counselling was given or not.* Every Christian is responsible before

the Lord for reading his or her Bible, especially the New Testament, and every Christian should be aware of the requirements of God regarding moral conduct, and the putting to death of the desires of the flesh (Gal. 5:24).

Failure to be obedient to the moral law of Christ in the New Covenant is therefore NOT a failure of the MINISTRY of deliverance, but a failure of the SUFFERER to be obedient to the Word of God. Any attempt by the unclean in the sufferer to blame their deliverance minister **for their own failures** should be strongly refuted and renounced.

(ii) FALSE EXPECTATIONS

Another situation of APPARENT failure occurs **when ministry is *successful* but *incomplete.*** The sufferer continues to complain of pressures and unclean desires and thinks "Oh, the ministry didn't work". How satan loves to take advantage of our ignorance and pull down the blessing of God. Adequate teaching should cover both these areas of so-called failure and present the true picture, which is that **thorough deliverance is not an "instant" ministry,** as so many think, and what we see as our "pollution" problem is really only the tip of the iceberg.

I have on my desk at the moment yet another leaflet advertising the ministry of an anointed evangelist-healer and it records the casting out of a snake spirit at one of his meetings. It reminded me that there are a number of evangelist-healers on the international circuit of ministry whose preaching is accompanied by signs and wonders, that is, healings, deliverances and other miracles. It is just like the Lord to confirm the preaching of the Kingdom of God with demonstrations of that Kingdom (Rule) but we need to remember that is what *signs* and wonders are - they are SIGNS or demonstrations that confirm the preaching (Mark 16:20, Acts 4:29-30, 1 Cor. 2:4).

They are not meant to be the end of the story or the end of the battle but the BEGINNING! Sometimes evangelists are understandably disappointed when they learn that many miracles at their meetings do not last - some last, many don't. Why? What is the Lord trying to say to us? I believe He is saying that a confirmation or a demonstration is exactly that - a demonstration of what CAN be if people move into the Kingdom of God through Christ, and began to exercise Kingdom *faith,* Kingdom *obedience* and Kingdom *living,* i.e., bring their lives into the order of the Rule of God. (Matt. 6:33, Rom. 15:18-19a, Heb. 2:4).

To expect Kingdom blessings to continue when those touched by the Lord are slipping back into the ways of the occult or the flesh (or perhaps they have never counted the cost to themselves and have never even renounced and forsaken the old ways) after the evangelist has gone home, is to misunderstand the will of God and to LOSE the blessing!

Signs and wonders are but a beginning, a taste of what CAN BE NORMAL **IF** we move into Kingdom living under the Lordship of Christ Jesus. If sickness and unclean habits return we should not lose heart but *understand* what the will of the Lord is for us today in this End-Time. **It is for total cleansing[1] and Christlikeness,** not just a patchwork, cosmetic miracle to some outward, visible problem such as polio, so that we can be "normalised" and go on our way to do what WE want, like the nine (9) lepers who did

---

[1] See **"End-Time Deliverance and the Holy Spirit Revival."**

not even take time to give thanks to the Saviour (Luke 17:11-19). There are ETERNAL things at stake and the Lord is not always going to bestow *permanent* healing on someone so that they can play the fool with eternal things. The physical and visible miracles are signs of an ETERNAL Kingdom of which we are invited to become members through the Cross of Christ Jesus. When we seek first the Kingdom or Rule of God and respond to the preaching of that Kingdom THEN temporal signs are often granted in order to confirm the truth of the eternal things preached by the Lord's servants (Mark 16:20, cf. Matt. 6:33).

Therefore the temporal or physical signs and blessings that people receive, AND THEIR PERMANENCY, are very much related to the people's relationship and attitude to the eternal Kingdom. We need to teach people who receive spiritual blessings to praise the Lord from the very beginning of their discovery of Him, and to give thanks in EVERY blessing AND problem (1 Thess. 5:18) so that, like the tenth leper, they can not only be cleansed from leprosy and cured but that they might also be SAVED, that is, experience a FULL salvation (v. 19). They need to be taught how to submit and draw near to God, AND resist the devil (James 4:7-8). When I say we need to teach people I am conscious that most experienced evangelists do their very best in Christ to establish new converts into the Kingdom of God - they really do - and failure to hold the blessing and grace of the Lord is very often *the sinners' and sufferers' failure* to renounce and forsake the old ways and really become new creatures in Christ (2 Cor. 5:17).

However the publicity of some evangelistic organisations leaves a lot to be desired. A very famous evangelist-healer visited Australia in 1986, a man who had preached in forty different countries around the world for more than forty years. This doyen of all evangelists described a shock he received before one of the public meetings. A group of two or three people pushing a person in a wheelchair caught him before the start of the meeting and said *"We have travelled all the way from... and we have to catch the next train back, leaving soon. Please pray for this person (in the wheelchair) and we'll be off".* The evangelist was stunned. As he recounted the story to his Australian listeners that evening he pleaded "Give us a chance!" He was shocked to think that people could believe that mighty miracles are performed in five minutes on an implied "guaranteed" and instant basis. But, of course, this is what many people think. Why? Perhaps because that is the way we understand the Bible and the ministry of Jesus and the apostles, and also perhaps because much of the publicity pouring out of the various evangelistic organisations gives an exaggerated and false picture of instant miracles occurring continuously, *and all the time.* In the noble desire to be positive and give glory to God, glowing reports are filed and ecstatic claims are made by the hundreds, *as if the battle was over and final victory won* so that everyone can live happily ever after.

Mighty healings are made to look so quick and easy, it is no surprise that readers think *"Hey, a couple of minutes prayer from you brother and we will catch the train home!"* And why should they not think this when all the publicity coming out of the evangelist's administration has conditioned them to think that way? The evangelist's problem is not with God's hungry and faithful people but with his own publicity.

Let us think for a moment. Signs are not an end in themselves. Signs are a BEGINNING and the battle is not over but has begun. The apostle Paul tells us that the power of

136

signs and wonders are for the purpose of winning the
OBEDIENCE OF THE NATIONS! (Romans 15:18-19a).

OBEDIENCE!
OBEDIENCE!
OBEDIENCE!

Not the half-hearted obedience that many Christians think
will keep them out of trouble with the Lord and in his blessings, but the kind of obedience that led the Son of God to
say **"I have come down from Heaven not to do my own
will, but the will of Him who sent me"** (John 6:38). I
suspect that if HALF the reports of COMPLETED healings
remained good, the nations of the earth would all be bow-
ing the knee to Jesus Christ NOW and not be the seething
cauldron of hate, spiritism, animism and anarchy they are
today. Some Christian publicity machines simply do not
always give us the true and full picture, partly because
they do not know it themselves, partly because they want
to glorify Christ, partly because they want to whip up interest and support, and partly because they have never understood where the *continuous* battle-lines are drawn in
the spiritual realm. They do not understand the damage
they are doing by encouraging people to believe that "easy,
instant blessing" is the only way to go. I almost added
"cosmetic" and "superficial" to those descriptions because
to me, even a healing from leprosy is cosmetic (Luke 17:11-
19) **when it is compared with eternal life** (Mark 9:43-47,
Luke 10:20). The bottom line is to be saved and OBEDI-
ENT to Christ is more important than to be cured even if
nine against one settle only for the physical healing. To be
saved for eternity means to be **obedient** (John 3:36,
Matt. 7:21, 24-27), **cleansed** (2 Cor. 7:1, 2 Tim. 2:21) **purified** (1 John 3:3, Matt. 5:8, James 4:8), **holy** (1 Peter
1:16), **perfect** (Matt. 5:48), **transformed** (Rom. 12:2), and

conformed to the image of the Son of God (1 John 3:2-3, Rom. 12:2).

Let us therefore make ourselves ready (Luke 3:4-9, Rev. 21:27, 19:7), because that is what **Deliverance and Restoration ministries** should be all about.

I believe I am right in saying that ninety-five percent of deliverance ministry today is only tip-of-the-ice-berg ministry, that is, incomplete! This is especially true in evangelistic crusades where the Lord encourages new believers with a blessed beginning, but expects them to FOLLOW THROUGH all the way!

(iii) MANIFESTATION-FREE DELIVERANCE

If you have read Book 1, you may remember my first abortive attempt at deliverance in **St. Stephen's Church, Penrith.** Nothing happened! No symptoms, no manifestations, nothing that I could SEE and so at that time I thought I had failed. But did I? I won't know the answer to that question until all things are revealed! As we wrote in 8.1 (iii) (b) there are many exits from the human body that can be used by unclean spirits - skin, anus, ears, nose, eyes etc., but there is only one that can make a lot of noise, and that is the MOUTH! Even then coughing and yawning, the most common forms of exiting, are not particularly noisy. It is only when a sufferer is getting loosed through retching or wailing etc., that the noise levels begin to rise. Today between seventy and eighty percent of people Verlie and I minister to show no obvious manifestations yet we know they are getting effective deliverance ministry because of the increase in our ability to discern this, that is, our ability to "know" the invisible action that is taking place. The sufferer may think the ministry has failed but we often know otherwise. If they can trust us (in the Lord) for a little while, they too will know the truth. Praise the Lord!

(iv) PARTIAL VICTORY

There is another "false failure", or incomplete ministry of which it is well to be warned. A lady who was very keen on the spiritual things of the Lord and assisted in deliverance at times, requested ministry for herself. She manifested powerfully and was released from quite a number of strong spirits - usually with four full-grown men hanging on to her (this was before we discovered how to use the Power of God). Early in ministry she was delighted and marvelled that one who was normally so weak (physically) would need so much restraining. Then her attitude changed and she refused to continue the ministry, saying that she didn't believe she had unclean spirits. When I reasoned with her that she should overrule the **"unbelief" spirit** in her and consider the enormous strength she manifested during sessions, she contradicted her earlier testimony and said that she had always been strong and her manifestations had been an act. I shared this new explanation with one of the men, a 15 stone six footer, and we marvelled together because many times we had hung on grimly during the battles and looked at each other with relief and joy when a spirit had departed. We knew the truth. In those days we did not know how to use our authority to the full or the Power of God, and unfortunately a successful ministry was cut short before victory could be completed. From the subject's point of view the ministry had been a failure because she now believed she had never needed it in the first place, but only thought she had. **Every battle we had been through together she dismissed in a single moment.** Let us all be warned of the fact that people who are receiving effective ministry can be mentally blocked by unbelief etc. and completely deny all that has happened - perhaps another good reason for obtaining written permission to minister. There was no failure of the ministry here, only a failure to appreciate what the Lord had done, and still wanted to do.

We nominate these as false failures because in each situation successful ministry was received but not pursued through to a visible and measurable victory.

9.2 OBVIOUS FAILURE OF THE SUFFERER

(i) DOUBLE-MINDEDNESS

An area of failure which cannot be blamed on the minister is caused by double-mindedness[1] of the sufferer. The sufferer says that he or she earnestly desires healing and deliverance and certainly one half of them is completely sincere in this. However, the truth may be that they are not fully committed to the Lord and they are not (yet) desperate enough for deliverance to yield to Jesus' Lordship unconditionally over their lives. Needless to say the unclean spirits will know this. They will know if you are ministering to somebody who lacks commitment and will be able to "dig their toes in" and hang in there against the ministry.

There have been a number of case histories illustrating this. Hilda flew up to Sydney one day from Melbourne with her "husband" and requested us to test him for certain demonic problems. There was no doubt from the counselling that there were problems in both their personalities and so we ended up ministering to both of them, but to no avail. Further counselling revealed that they were not married but living together in a "de facto" relationship and

---

[1] Literally "two-souled" (James 1:8. 4:8)

140

however acceptable that may be to the Governments and community of our day and age, it is not acceptable to Almighty God. As she was not sufficiently committed to the man to agree to marry him we could only send them home with a prayer for the future, saying "Sorry, we can't help you unless you are prepared to put your lifestyle right with Christ". But the Holy Spirit had not finished with them and we received a beautiful card of thanks a few days later telling us that the spirits had left them at Katoomba, a few miles out of Sydney, on the way home. Apparently they had made the right commitment and the spirits causing their immediate problems had left them both.

There was another case of a lass with a certain spirit we came to know as Mr Big because he was always very arrogant, telling us that he was there to stay. After we wrestled with Mr Big for weeks, the young lady finally admitted that she rather enjoyed having Mr Big and she wasn't really quite sure that she wanted to get rid of him. Incredible as it may seem this sort of thing is really quite common. Needless to say we didn't waste any more time with that case but left the door open for the lass to return should she come to a right mind in the matter.

There may not seem to be a great deal of difference between those who are double-minded and those who disregard the moral laws of Christ in the New Covenant. It seems to me that while both are causes for making the ministry ineffective, the double-minded person's problem is that of being deceived into doubt and procrastination, while the person who persists in living a lifestyle, knowing it to be displeasing to God, is exercising wilful rebellion. In either situation a decision of the will to choose the right and Godly course should change failure into success.

I do not doubt that you can think of other reasons why the

ministry may appear to fail because of the attitude or mis-understanding of the sufferer. Christians with **religious spir-its**[1] would be a major area of such failure. They can come into a deliverance meeting waving their arms about and ostentatiously praising the Lord, but their motives are not that of true praise, but to show how spiritual they are. They are not seeking the Lord's glory but their own!

(ii) ENEMY RELIGIOUS ESPIONAGE

Recently a rather disruptive lady came to our meetings and we were able to get victory over a number of rebel-lious and religious spirits which had tried to interfere with ministry to others by binding our anointing, especially that of Verlie, who is our deliverance minister. This attempt to interfere was followed by the use of Jesus' Name against us and I became filled with indignation for the honour of the Lord at what was tantamount to religious blasphemy and cried out, "How dare you foul spirits insult the Name of the Lord and insult the Lord's anointed ministers!"

The attacks on us immediately dried up and some releases obtained. In later clashes we were able to get past the unclean spirits to the human spirit in order to seek the woman's co-operation.

However when her HUMAN spirit declined to co-operate but sided with the unclean spirits within her we had no option but to cease ministry to her. It saddened us to real-ise that deep down she did not want to be cleansed but was simply a satanic agency sent to disrupt, hinder and destroy our ministry to others. Any unclean spirits we were successful in removing would make a speedy return to her

[1] Discussed in detail Book 4 **"Discerning Human Nature"**

as soon as she left the meeting, and further ministry would have been a waste of time and effort until she had a change of heart.

Such satanic agencies have been sent to us before and (P.T.L.) in the majority of cases the sufferer has turned the tables on satan and become a genuine disciple of the Lord, but when the HUMAN spirit *chooses* not to repent (change direction or purpose) then we exclude the person from ministry, at least until such time as we receive a request from them to re-join us IN WRITING, REPENTING and stipulating complete obedience and co-operation in future.

This is not done for our ego but for their salvation. We do not care how insulting, mocking or ugly *unclean spirits* become so long as the *sufferer* is trying to co-operate with Verlie and myself. The devil would love to deceive and play games with us, but as I have said before, we are too busy to play games, especially in matters of life and death.

Christians with religious spirits are often filled with the Holy Spirit also[1] and can be very acceptable to other Christians. However because an experienced deliverance ministry is just about the only part of the Body of Christ that can discern and expose some types of religious spirits, there can be quite a clash between minister and sufferer, with both claiming direct revelation by the Holy Spirit and using the Name of the Lord.

If the "religious" person then walks (or stalks) out[2] because they cannot accept exposure of their problem, that has to be labelled a failure of the sufferer.

---

[1] If this statement is confusing please refer to Book 1, Chapter 1 (vi)-(vii).
[2] See Book 2 Chapter 5, 3 (iv).

(iii) WRONG MOTIVES

Over the years we have noticed that the people who get the best results are the ones who already know they need deliverance and are looking for someone to minister it to them. The next most successful group are those who brought their problems to us and were able to accept that deliverance was the Lord's solution to their problems. Among the least successful were those who expected instant transformations so they could carry on their "normal" lives without difficulty, serving their own ambitions, and also those who had been ministered to by many other ministers beforehand. The attitude often was *"I've tried 'em all - no one has been able to help me"* and their faith level, especially for a program of ministry, was low to zero. One man was so lacking in motivation after only one deliverance session that he actually requested that I telephone him the night before the next meeting to remind him to come! I gently declined, and put it back on him to remember, thus saving us both from wasting our time.

I realise many fervent young Christians may be troubled by this, believing that every effort should be expended to help the demonised. However those of you who are experienced in counselling will have discovered the need for some level of effort or input from the sufferer whenever possible. The cries for help are so numerous that we have to have some way of distinguishing those genuinely calling upon the Name of the Lord (Psalm 143:6-7) from those who are playing games and would drain us spiritually and physically dry to no purpose.

There are, of course, many excuses available to sufferers for dropping out of any anointed, cleansing ministry and it is only the sufferers who want the perfect will of God for themselves who will persevere through to full victory and become part of the "wise virgins" (Matt. 25:1-13).

9.3   FAILURE OF THE MINISTER

Lack of training in spiritual warfare is almost always the reason for the failure of a ministry and this, of course, is very prevalent simply because specialist training in deliverance has not, to my knowledge, been widely available to student ministers. The Lord has had to train most deliverance ministers personally and privately, through fundamental Bible research and by trial and error, by success and failure, driving us back into the Word of God again and again. The training never seems to be completed, and some of us are thick-headed, with minds set in concrete and not as teachable as we would like to be. When we do have the opportunity to learn from other disciples we may be conscious that their teaching will need some adjustment when we apply it to our own ministry, because our knowledge of God and His unsearchable ways should never stand still or rest on the blessings of one of His servants of a previous day. One can sit down and analyse reasons for failures in the Church and of the Church, and such reasons may be very important to weigh and consider NOW, but the day is coming when the Power of God will be operating at such a level of activity[1] that a number of these comments about failures will no longer be relevant - Praise the Lord!

Continued failure of a ministry is most often due to **the minister's failure to use the spiritual weapons available to him from the Word of God.** Preparation by **prayer**

---

[1] Prophesied and written BEFORE the current so-called "Toronto Blessing" out pouring.

and fasting may be necessary to defeat tenacious spirits. Both these activities strengthen the spirit of the minister and reduce the hindrance of his flesh. He becomes spiritually strong and sensitive to the promptings of the Holy Spirit. His discernment is increased and he does not labour under the delusion that victory will always come easily or instantly. Because his flesh is subdued he expects to receive whatever Power of God and fulness is necessary and his faith becomes unwavering and rock-like. When weapons such as these are used the man of God is indeed a conquerer!

We have also mentioned other essential weapons, which we covered in our earlier studies - The **Power of God, Faith** to move mountains, understanding and exercising **Authority,** and **Discernment**[1]. I would like to add a little more detail to these in the context of this matter of failures.

(i) LACK OF DETERMINATION

Lack of Determination (which I view as synonymous with lack of FAITH or TRUST) in continuing battle can be described as a failure of the minister to win the day. This is where it can be important for large churches to develop and train a TEAM of deliverance ministers so that while some are in the front line and doing battle, others are on "stand by" as fresh reserves which can be thrown into the fray when the first line is pulled back for a break; and yet a third group is being refreshed and rested and strengthened with the Word of God, prayer and fasting etc. at home base. With this kind of suggested battle formation, deliverance ministers need not get over-tired, either spiritually or physically, and no battle need be lost through lack of

---

[1] Books 1 and 2

146

perseverance, because Faith or Trust is low. You will remember that the Lord's disciples failed on one occasion, **"Lord, why could we not cast it out?"** and they received "two" replies, which on closer examination may be described as one reply: (i) **"Because of your little faith"** (Matt. 17:20) and (ii) **"This kind come out by nothing except prayer and fasting"** (Mark 9:29) - "this kind" being an obvious reference to high-ranking spirits such as rulers and authorities. Prayer and fasting take time - they are part of battle preparations and they are entered into by soldiers of faith (not of little faith), soldiers who will never give up but who will persevere onto victory, perhaps not today, but next week or next month or even next year if necessary. **The victory of the Cross MUST become real[1] in our lives,** for the honour of the Lord as well as the salvation of the sufferer, so that *whilesoever the sufferer wishes to continue in faith and trust, so also must the minister.* Never give up. Never give up while the sufferer wants to continue, and the Lord will surely honour your faithfulness. But when we talk about perseverance in ministry, we do not normally mean long, long sessions, but a regular programme of sessions, perhaps on a weekly basis. We have already suggested that sessions without the context of worship should generally be no longer than one and a half hours (one hour is a suggested preference) except where extra-ordinary sessions, unrestricted by time or manpower and perhaps after prayer and fasting, have been deemed necessary.

"But Peter", you say, "How can you equate faith and trust in the Lord with persistent prayers and determined ministry? I always thought that trust was exercised when we Christians

---

[1] We must resist the devil UNTIL he flees from us (Jam. 4:7), and by so doing PROVE, that is, *experience* the perfect will of God (Rom. 12:2).

asked the Lord to do something and then we stop striving and let Him bring it to pass, believing that He will!"

The answer is that there ARE occasions when we ask and the Lord replies, "Leave it to me and I will work it out. Stand still and see the victory I am about to accomplish for you!" But such occasions are usually in the context of man's complete helplessness, when we have been obedient and done all that lies in our power in Christ to do. (Eph. 6:11,13) By such incidents the Lord gets glory for Himself for indeed *"man's extremity is God's opportunity"* when we are flowing in His perfect will.

However when the Lord has given US the weapons to use OURSELVES, in His Name, we dare not use the so-called Faith Position as a cop-out unless specifically directed by the Holy Spirit. In most situations we have NOT done all that lies in our power in Christ to do. In such circumstances the ceasing of ministry can be LACK of faith because we did not take up our spiritual weapons and use them until victory. In the book of Joshua the children of God are told to invade Canaan and go into battle - to be strong and of good courage - to have faith and trust - not to be afraid of the enemy but to GO IN! Today's End -Time challenge has much in common with the battles for the Promised Land.

2 Kings 13: 14 - 19   +   Psalm 68:30

David and Goliath

Standing still is NOT an act of faith in most instances of spiritual warfare - it takes faith to GO IN! It takes faith to pray and fast and to do battle until victory becomes reality. **Goliath** didn't fall over by himself or because an invisible angel of God gave him a push from behind. It took a **David** to step forward in the Name of his God to bring victory. And David was trained for that victory too. He had already stood up to defend his father's flocks with his life against wild beasts, and both lions and bears were slain in defence of the sheep (1 Sam. 17:33-37). It was no raw recruit in the Lord's Army that stood before the giant Goliath, but a young man who had been found faithful in the face of death in earlier battles. Too often we read the story of David and Goliath as if it were some romantic fairytale with easy victory coming on the spur of the moment. David had been tested and TRAINED by the Lord, and this is not in any way to minimise the courage and faithfulness of the young man.

Neither does David's part minimise the glory of the Lord for He declares that his forthcoming victory is so that *"all the earth may know that there is a God in Israel, and that all this assembly may know that the Lord does not deliver by sword or spear, for the battle is the Lord's ...."* (1 Sam. 17: 46- 47). The Lord used the faith and courage of a shepherd boy, and a slingshot. There will be times when the Lord will say, "Stand still and watch me" but this was not one of them.

Every campaign will be different but the battle is always the Lord's, whether He uses us or exercises His sovereignty in other ways. The important thing is to stay close and be in full communion, full fellowship with Him, available and girded for battle with our spiritual weapons at the ready. In the vast majority of situations we will be His David for today.

The Epileptic Boy

When we look at the incident of the deliverance and healing of **the epileptic, deaf and dumb lad** we find it contains a variety of *faith situations* which can teach us much:

1. The crowd's faith:

Jesus describes the crowd of people with whom He

deals as a "faithless generation" because one of them reports to Him that His disciples had failed to deliver the lad. Presumably this is a general comment aimed at the crowd at large, although not excluding His disciples (Mark 9:19).

2. The father's faith:

Jesus' conversation with the father of the boy reveals that *"all things are possible to him who believes."* The father then reveals his own state of confusion and double-mindedness, but together with those unhelpful qualities he reveals a sincere heart. He needs help to believe - and he asks for it - *"I believe; help my unbelief!"* The point is that *we (the sufferers) don't need a massive measure of mature faith in order to receive answered prayers,* BUT the one to whom we appeal - the minister of God - must be strong in faith in order to *give* whatever ministry is required. (Mark 9:23-24).

3. The disciples' faith:

When the disciples asked Jesus privately why they could not cast out the spirit(s) and heal the boy, the Lord gave them the double-sided answer we have noted, including, **"Because of your little faith."** They may not have encountered such strong opposition before and had given up too easily, not understanding that prayer and fasting would be necessary.

Whichever way we look at it we have to acknowledge that *the only variable in this situation is the ministry.* The problem remained the same for both the disciples and the Lord. The faith of the father was just basic, seed faith - nothing to get excited about - but the difference lies in the ministers. The disciples had Jesus' authority to use His Name, just like we have today - but failed. *The difference between the ministry of the disciples and the ministry of the Lord Himself is clear for all to see.* Now answer this question honestly. How many ministers (disciples) today would have laid the blame for failure back onto **poor old dad**?

Sometimes we Pastors outsmart ourselves with philosophical "gobbledegook" on faith for sufferers. We make it into a monstrous intellectual doctrine so that we can blame people for lacking it, but in so many cases this so-called "lack of faith" is patently untrue. I once sat in the lounge room of a Christian lady whose faith would warm any Pastor's heart. She gave a glowing, positive testimony of how the Lord had healed her, in total contradiction of the physical evidence, which was that she was crippled with multiple sclerosis and had been a sufferer for many years. As I felt my heart respond to her declaration, I determined that, by God's grace, we would bring upon her the authority and power of the risen Christ in response to that faith, so that her declaration becomes real in the flesh! But for this to happen she - and we - must be DOERS of the Word, not hearers and readers only.

There are thousands of Christians throughout the world who are continuing to suffer for months, even years, pretending that they are healed or delivered because they think that is all that is neccssary to obtain what they want. Jesus doesn't say pretend, but trust (believe), *seek* and tell me the TRUTH and I'll bring the *power of God* to bear on the situation, for in spiritual warfare we are kept safe, guarded and preserved by THE POWER OF GOD THROUGH FAITH (TRUST) (1 Peter 1:5). This trust is not passive, but it means *"trust in battle"*, because it looses the power of God.

The "FAITH POSITION" ought never to be an escape hatch for those who are reluctant to enter into spiritual warfare for the Lord's glory. It is not helpful saying, *"I trust in the Lord for that problem"* twenty times a day if you never take up your spiritual weapons of authority and power, etc. and fight for the victory, that is, unless you have first done ALL in your power, in Christ. (Eph. 6:11,13).

(ii) LACK OF DISCERNMENT

We have already written about the gift of discerning of spirits. Taking this one step further, there are some fine Christians who hold the Faith Position and who believe in exercising the ministry of deliverance but they use their weapons only briefly, and put them down again, because they believe in issuing one, or two commands at the most, *"Loose him in Jesus' Name"* and then they stop. They want the sufferer to hold a position of FAITH, standing on a part of the Word of God, believing that they HAVE BEEN DELIVERED (in the spiritual realm) no matter what symptoms of pain and discomfort may continue to be manifested in the sufferer. I find in this presentation of the deliverance ministry a very subtle distortion indeed because it contains so much that is good and true, but it is often inadequate. Symptoms DO matter-contrary to much current theological teaching - especially when they are manifestations of warfare. Let me say that again - SYMPTOMS DO MATTER! It is true the Bible tells us repeatedly to believe (trust) in the Lord Jesus. It tells us to look to Jesus and all the other positive things like taking the battle into the spiritual realm where we can always win, and out of the realm of the flesh where we often lose, *but it does NOT tell us to always ignore the symptoms in our flesh.* Why? Because it is these very symptoms which manifest the conflict taking place (Mark 8:22-25), and if only we ministers can learn to "read" the evidence correctly, by God's Spirit, the quicker the sufferer will be restored to health.

We have to learn to discern whether symptoms mean that:

(a) *The infirmity is coming out, in accord with our prayers and commands,* and is simply causing some temporary pain or discomfort as it surfaces in the soul and removes itself from bone and flesh. With this situation the Faith position may prove to be adequate and obtain the healing or deliverance expected, but I believe that **persistent**, anointed ministry will sometimes obtain quicker and deeper cleansing. Flesh symptoms in this situation can be rebuked, ignored or a cause for praise.

or (b) *The infirmity is stirred up, and like a scorpion is preparing to fight tenaciously* in order to hold its position in the body. It can make the life of the sufferer miserable, even for years, without yielding up its grip. In this case the so-called "Faith position" with its single command theory is usually quite unable to achieve the required healing, except possibly over a protracted period of suffering. The battle simply goes on and on, and the sufferer learns to live with it until something or someone gives way. What is required here is a **persistent** attack against the enemy with all the *authority and power of the risen Christ,* and once we are committed into battle we should never concede defeat. Whilesoever the sufferer is prepared to "soldier on" in spiritual warfare and fight the good fight against their affliction we who minister must stand with them side by side. We will learn so much if we do this, and what the Lord teaches us when the going gets tough is just so much more valuable than all the theoretical doctrines we learn from books. The minister who prays once over every sufferer and then takes refuge in the so-called "Faith" position can never learn what God wants to teach him, because praying once is not always a true exercise of faith (trust) but sometimes it can mask an unwillingness to go to war.

Sufferers should always be taught to have a positive confession of what God has done, and is doing, in the Spirit but that should not prevent them from being totally honest about the symptoms they experience in the flesh, so long as they are not manifesting unclean spirits of negativity, self pity and attention seeking etc. *It is the spirit* behind the confession that is important.

Likewise those who minister should not rebuke sufferers who tell them the truth in good spirit, but rather MAINTAIN THE MINISTRY. When the going gets tough, the tough get going! Remembering always that we are strong *in the Lord* and in the strength of His might (Eph. 6:10).

(c) *A third and very strong possibility is that* if the symptoms manifesting and causing distress continue without any change for better or for worse after ministry, *we are on the wrong track.* Lack of discernment of the *real* problem i.e. the SPIRITUAL enemy behind the PHYSICAL enemy is the most common cause of delay or failure by far! Maybe the Lord wants some deeper, hidden causal problem attended to before the more obvious problems can be ministered to successfully. Here is where we need to ask the Lord for discernment.

154

> The great lesson for ministers is, "Don't ignore the symptoms like spiritual blind men do, but *read and understand them,* and press on to victory in Jesus' Name!"

An insufficiently developed gift of discerning of spirits is therefore a major cause of ministry failure. For the most part people will tell you their basic and obvious areas of weakness, especially what is troubling them, and as your deliverance counselling experience grows so will your discernment[1] (Heb. 5:13-14) so you will know in your spirit what is the troublesome spirit in the sufferer before you are told. Always tackle the unclean spirits revealed to you by the Holy Spirit FIRST, because that is why they have been shown to you. Others will be revealed later because the Lord wants you to attack them later. Operate on the spiritual level rather than the mind level and let the Lord direct the battle tactics. If you exercise deliverance to your OWN battle plan you may well meet with a spiritual brick wall. The Lord knows the way to break down the kingdom of darkness in a person - stone by stone if necessary - and His way is the best way.

There is no short cut to experience and that is another reason why it is a good idea to train a team, with team members working together with an experienced person for some time before operating unsupervised, always subject to the leading of the Spirit and circumstances.

Elisha and the Shunammite

In the story of the deliverance and raising to life of the **Shunammite woman's son**, a number of features help us (2 Kings 4:25-37).

---

[1] See Chap. 3,6 - Book 1

(i)   **Elisha** has **Gehazi** as his trainee assistant and sends him to enquire from the woman when he sees her approaching (v.26).

(ii) Gehazi tries to protect Elisha from the woman's vexed attention, but Elisha wants to hear the problem from the woman's lips BECAUSE THE LORD WITHHELD DIS-CERNMENT OR KNOWLEDGE of it from the prophet.

It is important for us all to remember that discernment, although it can be trained and matured, is not a gift that operates purely at OUR discretion.[1] The Lord either gives it or withholds it, as in this case (v.27), so that the woman can be heard.

Recently a Christian lady asked for an interview with Verlie and myself as she had been along to a couple of meetings. However Verlie discerned that her motives were not pure and declined to be present.

When the lass arrived she was very disappointed that Verlie was absent and wanted to know what we both had discerned about her. I tactfully explained that we had received enough discernment to make an effective start on her cleansing but that it was not normal for us to divulge very much of what the Lord had shown us. As a matter of fact I had not been given much definitive information on her at all and I perceived that the Lord had withheld a great deal because the lass was really more curious about herself - wanting information that SHE could verify (a kind

---

[1] Discernment is fully dependant on the HOLY Spirit, because it is God operating sovereignly through the Christian. The discretion is totally God's. Alternatively gifts of Tongues, Preaching etc. are different in that they are operated by the HUMAN spirit, albeit aided by the Holy Spirit (1 Cor. 14:14). Therefore they can operate by human choice or will and are normally always available for use.

of miracle-chasing) and agree with rather than genuinely desiring a good clean out. Even some of the few things I shared she could not accept so we were really wasting each other's time. THE LORD KNOWS OUR HEARTS, AND REVEALS OR NOT, ACCORDINGLY.

(iii) The servant Gehazi is directed to go and minister to the woman's son (v.29) but fails (v.31).

(iv) After Elisha's ministry the child sneezes out the problems, probably **death and infirmity spirits** (v.35).

One either sees things in the spiritual realm by the Holy Spirit or one does not. I suggest that those who do not see, act with wisdom when seeking to instruct those who do. Better to say nothing until you know what you are talking about.

There are two basic failures possible in exercising discernment. They are failure to discern:

(i) the CHARACTER of the spirit, e.g. resentment, hatred, fear etc., and;

(ii) the NAME of the spirit (e.g. Legion, Python). Legion was the name of a spirit cast out by Jesus and it manifested a character of violence, destruction and insanity, while Paul cast out the spirit of a python from a girl which enabled her to practice occult powers of divination, clairvoyance and fortune-telling. (Acts 16:16-18).

We can come against the CHARACTER manifested by spirits such as these today and still enjoy considerable success. We can usually make huge dents in the kingdom of satan simply by naming the character we want to cast out - **"Clairvoyance, come out in Jesus name!"** - but how much more effective we would be in *difficult* sessions of ministry if we knew the NAME. We will often be resisted when we command a spirit to name itself but *sometimes* it is necessary to obtain the name if we are to experience total, or even partial, victory. So how do we get the spirit's name if it is stubbornly resisting our command to name itself? Obviously it can be revealed through the revelational gifts of knowledge and discernment direct from the Lord (1 Cor. 12:8-10) and this is what happens.

My wife Verlie rarely demands that a spirit name itself, and that is because in our group meetings she is always given so many names and characters direct from the Lord that she has her hands full dismissing those. Occasionally she will say to me in private that she hasn't quite got the name of a spirit in so-and-so and then in the Lord's timing it comes through. I BELIEVE THAT JESUS' CLASH WITH LEGION HAPPENED THAT WAY, NOT BECAUSE IT WAS ESSENTIAL THAT EVERY DEMON BE NAMED, BUT TO SHOW US HOW PERSONALISED THE BATTLE CAN BE-COME, AND THE COMPLEXITY AND PLURALITY OF SPIRITS UNDER A SINGLE NAME!

Lack of discernment is therefore a major cause of ministry failure. Strong or difficult spirits may not move out at a command addressed simply to unclean spirits, but to char-acterise them or to name them is to expose them and have authority over them (1 Cor. 12:10, Mark 5:9).

And remember, wherever we start, it is usually **only the tip of the iceberg!**

(iii) LACK OF AUTHORITY

We have already seen a glimpse of the authority given to mankind and it is so staggering that we find it hard to realise its full significance- **"over *all* the power of the enemy"** and **"whatever you bind** (present and future) **on earth having been bound** (past tense continuing to the present) **in heaven, shall be** (future tense)" (Matt. 16:19 lit. Greek). This latter reference does not, of course, give Christians a blank cheque with authority to order their every whim, as some think (1 John 5:14), but it does say that whatever we bind or loose on earth - provided it is in accord with the mind of Christ and is thus *already bound or loosed in heaven -* shall come to pass. This is mind-blowing indeed but **Paul** adds even more to our Christian weaponry by writing:

"For walking in (the) *flesh, we* (make) *war not according to* (the) *flesh, for the weapons of our warfare* (are) *not fleshly but powerful by God to overthrow strongholds, overthrowing reasonings* (thoughts, imaginations, philosophy, intellectualism) *and every high* (ranking) *thing rising up against the knowledge of God, and taking captive every mind* (thought, purpose) *for the obedience of Christ, being ready to punish every disobedience,* **when your obedience is fulfilled"** (2 Cor. 10:3-6 lit. Greek with added words in brackets).

Did you know that when you have:

(i) understood your authority in Christ, and
(ii) fulfilled your own obedience to Christ

then you can trample all over the logic of satan and indeed any spiritual foe trying to prevent the knowledge of God?

OBEDIENCE!
OBEDIENCE!
OBEDIENCE!

Did you know you can take captive the human mind for obedience to (and the glory of) Christ? The polluted mind-control that satan imposed on us all, in the past, can be broken - hallelujah! I didn't say it (first) - Paul did. It's in the Word of God. Do you believe it? Would you like to try and make the scripture say something else a little less controversial? - Well, that is why we have spelt it out in the original Greek for you. Even remove the bracketed words if you like and see if you can make the passage mean something else, in good conscience. When we stop to think about it, we realise that evangelists do this all the time when they bring unforgiven sinners to repentance, that is, cause them to change their minds and the direction of their lives towards obedience to Christ.

I think you will end up agreeing that we have been given a spiritual weapon of great magnitude which can be used in all manner of warfare - praise the Lord - that of AUTHORITY TO TAKE CAPTIVE AND TO OVERTHROW any form of enemy opposing the truth of Christ Jesus IF (and it is a big IF) we are prepared to use it.

Moses had to learn how to use the authority that God had given him when leading the Israelites out of Egypt. The Israelites were encamped against the sea and the vengeful Egyptians were closing in on them fast to destroy them. Moses told the people,

> *"Do not be afraid. Stand still and see the salvation of the Lord, which He will show to you today for the Egyptians whom you have seen today, you shall never see them again. The Lord shall fight for you and you shall hold your peace." (Exod. 14:13-14).*

I can hear many believers saying, "Terrific, the Lord will surely be pleased with such faith, for the battle is His, He is going to do it, and all we have to do is watch." That may have been true from the point of view of the Israelites but *it was not true for Moses who was invested with God's authority (as we Christians are today)*. God then said to him,

> **"Why do you cry to me? (You) Speak to the children of Israel that they go forward: but (you) lift up your rod and stretch out your hand over the sea, and divide it: and the children of Israel shall go on dry ground through the midst of the sea...."** (Exod. 14:15-16).

To paraphrase this the Lord is saying, "Don't tell me the problem any more, I know it. **Use the authority I have given you!**"

I vividly remember an incident where I was suffering great pain in my stomach which reached a point where a shooting stab of pain seemed to cut me in half and I collapsed as if pole-axed onto the floor. During this attack I had been crying out to the Lord to deliver me. As I lay on the floor in agony I heard the Lord say within me "USE YOUR AUTHORITY!" I immediately rebuked the spirit of infirmity attacking me and commanded it to go in Jesus' Name. The pain ceased abruptly. It was the quickest healing I have ever experienced.

There will be times when the Lord will heal without needing anything more than a request in order to show His sovereign power, but speaking in general terms for the times in which we live He is far more likely to say, "Why do you cry to me? **Use your authority!**"

(iv) LACK OF POWER

When the blind man had been ministered to by the Lord

Jesus, he was asked, "What do you see?" He replied, "I see men as trees, walking". So Jesus ministered to him again and the blind man clearly saw. (Mark 8:22-25). Many preachers would tell us that the blind man should have been told *"I have ministered to you - now don't worry that things are a bit blurred - just trust. Ignore any remaining symptoms of blindness - pretend they are not there and whatever you do don't admit to them because if you do you won't get better. Confess with your mouth that you see perfectly clearly and as you confess your healing you will be healed."* Am I being too harsh if I say that this kind of well-meaning Christian advice is often an extraordinarily subtle way of getting Christians to confess or **say something that is not true,** in the belief that saying something makes it happen or become true. If the blind man had said to Jesus after the first stage of the ministry, "I see everything clearly" the Lord may not have ministered an increase of healing power to him to complete the healing. **It is good to have a positive confession, so long as it is TRUE!**

This in no way contradicts what we have expressed in "Your Confession of Faith" (7.3 (iii) (f)2) regarding the importance of confessing our faith, which is the confession of our LEGAL position in Christ, *the reality of things hoped for, the conviction (proof) of things not (yet) seen (Heb. 11:1).*

There is a time to declare out loud our LEGAL position into the SPIRITUAL realm, and there is a time to declare the REALITY of our PHYSICAL condition, to the Lord or the Lord's minister to you.

A key teaching from the Lord helps make this clear:

> **"Have the faith of God.** *Truly I tell you that whoever says to this mountain 'Be taken and cast into*

the sea', and does not doubt in his heart but be-
lieves that what he says happens, it will be done
for him."

(Mark 11:22-23,-literal).

"But", you say, "Surely this text disproves your point?" Not
really. As I said a moment ago, I am all for positive confession AS LONG AS IT IS TRUE! Please note that **the above
text is not just a FAITH text but it is also an AUTHOR-
ITY text.** It tells me that:

(a) when I EXERCISE my authority as a Christian (which
     comes from the Word of God), and
(b) because I am MINISTERING in Jesus' Name and
(c) believing with the FAITH that God alone can give me,
     because HIS will is MY will, that
(d) all the POWER of the Godhead is backing me, then
(e) that which I have declared authoritatively in Jesus'
     Name will HAPPEN, even to commanding a mountain
     to be moved and cast into the sea!

Obviously the power of God flows when we are completely
in tune with the mind of Christ and minister accordingly.
Ministers are utterly dependant upon the Lord to be present
to execute His Word of authority by the touch of His Spirit,
in every ministry situation.

During World War II an elderly lady was seen constantly
waiting on the wharves of Sydney Harbour. When an ob-
servant bystander noticed her there day after day as various ships came and went, and enquired who she was, he
was told that her son had been killed in World War ONE,
more than twenty years before. She had been unable to
accept her loss and had continued to wait patiently for her
son to disembark for twenty years, believing him to be still
alive in the flesh.

This sad story has a message for us. She could think, dream, pretend, speak it out, believe, and ask God until she was blue in the face, but the sad truth was that this poor woman was deluded and could not receive the truth. No doubt she exercised faith but it was not the faith OF God, because that is only granted so that we may perform the WILL of God. Her "faith" came from the imagination of her heart, and WAS NOT BASED ON THE WORD OF GOD!

When we can accept the TRUTH, and Jesus is the Truth, we begin to move into the WILL of God and we find that the indwelling Christ imparts HIS faith to us. So I put it to you that believing in your heart what you say will be done for you is only spiritually and physically valid IF you **"have the faith of God." If you take away these first five words** that Jesus spoke from our quoted scripture text, **then every word that follows can be twisted out of its real meaning**, and bring about presumption rather than power.

Jesus' words do NOT tell me that a positive mental (soulish) attitude in the fashion of the world's sales empires will bring down the power of God; they do NOT tell me that wishful thinking, dreaming, pretending or even speaking things into being ALONE will bring down the power of God, and give effect to what I want, but they tell me that faith (TRUST) inspired of God, coupled WITH AUTHORITY SPOKEN out and inspired of God, will produce the POWER to achieve the purposes of GOD, even to the moving of mountains.

Also **"speaking things into being" does not mean an ordinary conversational speaking of what is required.** That may work when your problems are controlled by weakish spirits but if your problems are controlled by rulers and authorities you will need to speak things out WITH AUTHORITY. There is a rank of spirit whose power can only be broken by prayer and fasting and **Jesus' words are for those who minister rather than for those who seek ministry.** They speak of a dynamic active faith rather than a "I'll stand over here while I hope you do it" kind of passive faith.

Neither does this Scripture passage (Mark 11:22-23) in any way remove the need for the POWER of God. That is why so many brethren become disappointed with poor results! They have been taught that just speaking things out makes things happen, regardless of **faith in the heart,** or **authority in the voice.** Even those who do receive their desires, so often have to wait for weeks, months, and even years, to obtain their answers. Why? Because they have not understood that this verse is given as a **basis for authority** so that power can flow. They do not use their authority and they wonder why there is no power flowing to make the things that they ask for come to pass.

When we ask people (for whom we are praying or casting out demons in Jesus' Name) about their condition, we expect them to tell us the TRUTH, e.g. whether they can see; whether they can hear; what emotions they feel. We don't want to hear what they THINK we want to hear – some "pious", deceitful platitude about feeling great – UNLESS they DO feel great! We want them to speak it as it is but without self-pity, guilt, condemnation or any unclean negativity or attention-seeking. Let them tell the truth with a good and expectant conscience like the blind man's *"I see men as trees, walking".*

This, in itself, was a positive comment of truth about his progressive healing. He wasn't filled with self-pity, negativity or unbelief – those attitudes are spiritual and MUST be changed when they seek to manifest – neither did he attempt to deceive the Lord by saying he was healed. He told it like it was, in a positive, expectant way, according to his physical symptoms, and then the Lord completed His gracious work.

If we exercise faith and authority and then find that no physical results are at present forthcoming, we ought not to fall into the trap of (always) blaming the sufferer for lack of faith. It may be that lack of POWER is the problem and the minister needs to look to himself and ask for a greater anointing from above upon His ministry, while MAINTAINING THE MINISTRY to the sufferer. If the Lord Jesus Christ needed to minister more healing power to the blind man (even with His mighty anointing), how much more should we learners (disciples) need to do so at times.

Only Believe?

"But" you say, "in the incident where Jesus raised Jairus' daughter from the dead Jesus told Jairus not to be afraid but ONLY BELIEVE (Mark 5:36). That is ALL we have to do - only believe! Right?" WRONG! *It all depends whether you are the one receiving or the one giving ministry!* After He spoke those words Jesus as minister acted as He would want us to act in His Name today. He went to the house and removed all the mourners. Then He went to the child's corpse and took her by the hand and said, "Damsel, I say to you, Arise." "But" you say, "If I tried that with a corpse it wouldn't work" and you are probably right. What then is the difference? IT IS THE POWER OF GOD! It is written of Jesus that "the power of the Lord was with Him to heal." *When the power of the Lord is with us to heal like it was with Jesus then we will be able to do what Jesus did.* WE will be able to say "Only believe" to people in need because we will be able to minister the power of God in response to the faith of the sufferer and obtain victory in Jesus' Name. The key to remember is that we Christians are not kept (guarded, preserved) by faith but by THE POWER OF GOD THROUGH FAITH (1 Peter 1:5) in spiritual warfare. SOME FAILURES HAVE LITTLE TO DO WITH THE LACK OF FAITH OF THE SUFFERER AND MORE TO DO WITH THE LACK OF POWER OF GOD THROUGH THE MINISTER[1] - sad, but true, but praise the Lord this situation is changing TODAY, by the grace of God. It is true that the SUFFERER is required to "only believe (trust)" but the MINISTER needs the anointing of the POWER[2] of God for victory.

Is it any wonder that the good Lord had to sovereignly pour out the so-called **"Toronto Blessing"**[3] to get (some) churches moving into cleansing and preparing for the Trumpet of God (1 Thess. 4:16). And even now (as I write) many churches don't know how to build on this Revival. Others vigorously oppose it, especially those without any deliverance experience, being unaware that **it is a salvation ministry obtained through the blood sacrifice of the Son of God.**

It just goes to show what a mess the church(es) can get themselves into when they fail to fully carry out the Great Commission (Matt. 10:1 with 28:20). See 10.4 ahead.

While acknowledging the reality of failures, it is as well to remember that the New Testament has a lot to say about **endurance** and **perseverance.** I saw a sign in a newspaper shop the other day which showed me that even the world

---

[1] But see the earlier part of this chapter in order to balance this comment with ALL the possible causes of failure.
[2] See **"Christian Authority and Power"** for a more detailed explanation, and how to grow in your anointing and power from the Lord.
[3] See **"Toronto and the Truths You Need to know"**.

can borrow a slogan right out of the Christian ethic, something which expresses the certain hope of Christians **everywhere.**

"YOU HAVE NOT FAILED UNTIL YOU GIVE UP!"

CHAPTER 10

PURPOSE OF DELIVERANCE

10.1 EVIDENCE OF THE KINGDOM OR RULE OF GOD

(i)   Jews under the Old Covenant

Under the Old Covenant the Hebrew people of God saw things in a very practical way. Salvation was thought of in terms of being saved or delivered from the hands of the physical, pagan enemies they could see with their physical eyes. For the most part Heaven and/or the Kingdom of God appeared to be the promised land of Canaan and in particular Zion and the city of Jerusalem. The future hope of (Eternal) Life was achieved by having children and grandchildren and great grandchildren in order that your NAME should live on after your death. Only here and there (in the Law and the Prophets) did the devout Jew see or understand the Scriptures he was taught as referring to Life after death in a Heavenly "country". He lived under the Old Covenant which is described as "ordinances of the flesh" (Heb. 9:10 Col. 2:20-22) and understandably could scarcely perceive the future things of the Spirit, in his own time.

Consequently when the Messiah came and told them of SPIRITUAL things it was no wonder that the Jewish people lacked the spiritual perception necessary to "see" (John 9:39-41). If we were correct when we drew a parallel between Joshua's casting out of the Canaanites from the Promised Land and the casting out of demons today,[1] then

---

[1] Book 2 Chap. 6.1 (iii)

170

it follows that salvation and/or the Kingdom of God under the **Old** Covenant was seen in physical, fleshly well-being, while we who live in the light of the **New** Covenant are strongly exhorted to walk in the Spirit. The age of the Spirit has been HERE since Pentecost but, like those Jews who hardened their hearts, we are beset by a spirit of stupor (Rom. 11:8) that persists in trying to keep us in the realm of the flesh (satan's territory). This spirit seeks to prevent us from elevating ourselves into the spiritual realm where we may focus on spiritual things as they really are, able to know our friends from our enemies, able to distinguish between self-will and the will of the Lord, for we do not contend with flesh and blood but with spiritual rulers and authorities.... (Eph. 6:12).

(ii)   The Ministry of John the Baptist

The Baptist, because he belongs to the Old Testament line of prophets, had a straight preaching and warning role, apparently without any accompanying or confirming signs. His message was *"Repent, for the Kingdom of Heaven is at hand"* (Matt. 3:2) which, being interpreted, means "Express or experience a Godly grief for your sins and radically change the direction of your lives towards Godliness, for the Rule of God over your lives is at hand."

The Baptist also preaches "Repent" like the Old Testament prophets before him (and the Apostles after him) and he comes in the spirit of Elijah but he uses a new term "The Kingdom of Heaven (or God)" which we understand today to mean the Rule or Realm of God - more of a spiritual relationship rather than a geographical place.[1] His ministry is unique in that it is preparatory for the coming of the

---

[1] See Book 2 Chap. 6.1 (iv)

Messiah and as such his message is for a particular time in God's timetable. It belongs to the New Testament age of the Spirit while at the same time it follows in the tradition of MOST of the Old Testament prophets by the absence of accompanying signs or miracles, deliverance and healing.

(iii) The Ministry of Jesus

Because deliverance is a SALVATION ministry its source is found in the Saviourhood of Jesus Christ and consequently is prominently manifested in Jesus' own earthly ministry. When Jesus appears on the earthly scene ready to commence ministry He preaches the same message as John the Baptist, *"Repent for the Kingdom of Heaven is at hand"* (Matt. 4:17) but immediately we notice in the same context there is a significant change - and addition - as Jesus went about *"....preaching the gospel of the Kingdom and healing every disease and infirmity... demoniacs"* etc. (Matt. 4:23-24, cf 9:32-36).

It is evident that the miracles of salvation of the soul and flesh by deliverance and healing are a DEMONSTRATION of the sovereign rule of God through Christ. When John the Baptist, while languishing in prison queried (through his disciples) whether Jesus really was The Christ, the New Testament records that -

> "In that hour He cured many of diseases and plagues and evil spirits and on many that were blind He bestowed sight. And He answered them, 'Go and tell John what you have seen and heard, the blind receive their sight, the lame walk, lepers are cleansed and the deaf hear and the dead are raised up, and the poor have the good news preached to them, and blessed is he who takes no offence in Me.'" (Luke 7:20-23).

172

Isn't that staggering? What answer does the Lord Jesus give him? He doesn't turn around and say to him, "Oh I am really the Christ you know. I can't really prove it to you at the moment, but if you have faith and take my word for it, hold on, you will be okay, and the Will of God will be worked out in your life." No, it's not an answer of words at all, but it is an answer of *DEEDS.* It is an answer of *POWER* (1 Cor. 4:20). It is an answer of the demonstration of the Kingdom of God (Heb. 2:14). For indeed as Jesus said, *"If I by the finger of God (or by the Spirit of God) cast out demons then has the Kingdom of God come upon you."* (Luke 11:20, Matt. 12:28). The preaching of the Gospel of the Kingdom of God is sealed by the power of God, by signs and wonders (Rom. 15:18-19), and that is the answer Jesus sent back to John the Baptist languishing in prison. The quality of the mighty miracles demonstrate that God's Anointed has come, and that the King had brought upon them the Kingdom of God (cf. Heb. 2:3-4).

(iv) The Ministry of the Disciples

The ministry of Jesus is carried on by the disciples in obedience to the Lord's commands to preach and to say *"The Kingdom of Heaven is at hand".* They are to *"heal the sick, raise the dead, cleanse lepers, cast out demons,"* etc. (Matt. 10:7-8, cf. Luke 9:1-2, 10:9). It is very clear that the preaching of the Gospel of the Kingdom and the casting out of demons go hand in hand for the disciples also. Why? Because *the miracles confirm or seal the preached Word* (Mark 16:20). The Early Church prayed *"And now Lord, look upon their threats, and grant to your servants to speak the Word with all boldness while you stretch out your hand to heal, and signs and wonders are performed through the name of your Holy Servant, Jesus".* (Acts 4:29-30). Isn't that tremendous? Now if the Early Church can pray with such faith and expectancy, so can we, and when we minister a genuine ministry of deliverance in Jesus' Name today, we should understand it demonstrates that the Kingdom or Rule of God has come upon us, displacing the kingdom of satan.

It is sometimes argued that we cannot ALWAYS take the Lord's commands to his disciples and lay them as burdens upon today's Christians, because if we did, we would have to raise the dead and go forth into the world without staff, wallet, bread, money, purse and carrying no shoes or a second coat (Luke 9:3, 10:4). But the answer to that objection is Christians with faith in the risen Christ and His Word *DO* raise the dead today **(Archbishop Benson Idahosa** testifies to six (6) such occasions in his ministry), and also the instructions not to take certain gear on missionary's journeys was **retracted** by the Lord[1] prior to His crucifixion (Luke 22:35-36). Apparently the missionary journeys of the twelve and the seventy were training ventures, not only in (i) the exercise of the power of God over sickness, demonisation and death, but also training in (ii) believing for God's supply of every physical need AND (iii) the humility to RECEIVE their daily needs in return for ministry given - not always an easy thing for honourable men to learn. The Lord's retraction of these earlier directions to the disciples to take nothing with them is not meant to indicate that God's supply is any less, but rather that with the gathering of the black clouds of the powers of darkness for the warfare soon to result in the Crucifixion and beyond, every disciple would need to exercise all the gifts and weapons at his or her disposal, both SPIRITUAL AND PHYSICAL, in order to be overcomers. Not the least of these gifts is wisdom - they are to be wise as serpents and harmless as doves! Since the time of the Crucifixion the warfare has been in small measure directed BY US but

[1] See pp. 98-100

174

mostly UPON US (today's disciples). Today we are turning this around because it is the Church of God that should be attacking and besieging the gates of Hades, and prevailing (Matt. 16:18). Praise the Name of the Lord!

Let us summarise:

In these days of spiritual conflict, frantic satanic activity and widespread unbelief the Lord is gracious to add confirming signs to validate the preaching of the King (Jesus) and the Kingdom of God. It is not that gospel preaching NEEDS signs, for the Holy Spirit will blow where He wills, but in the sovereignty and providence of God signs DEMONSTRATE the kingdom presented by preaching. Such demonstrations are a seal from God on the preached Word, for **the Kingdom of God consists not in talk (word) but in POWER (1 Cor. 4:20).**

10.2 TO SET THE CAPTIVES FREE

The ministry of deliverance is an exercise of the compassion of Jesus on the multitudes of the lost sheep. It was after preaching and teaching, healing and delivering that Jesus said, *"the harvest is great but the labourers are few, pray (ye) the Lord of the harvest to send forth labourers..."* As we look at the context of that passage (Matt. 9:35 - 10:16, but don't take any notice of the unfortunate chapter division, drawn by men), we notice the tremendous sense of compassion that Jesus had for those to whom He ministered:

> *"And Jesus went about all the cities and villages, teaching in their synagogues and proclaiming the gospel of the Kingdom and healing every disease and every illness.*

*And seeing the crowds he **WAS MOVED IN HIS EMOTIONS** concerning them because they were distressed and helpless, as sheep without a shepherd.*

*Then He said to his disciples, the harvest is great, but (in contrast) the labourers (are) few, pray therefore the Lord of the harvest so that He **SENDS OUT** workers into His harvest.*

*And He called to Him His twelve disciples and gave to them authority over unclean spirits so as to cast them out, and to heal every disease and every illness .... These twelve Jesus **SENT OUT ....**" (Matt. 9.35 -10:5 literal).*

The verb often translated "compassion" or "pity" in verse 36 means literally to be "moved with emotion in the inward parts" which can mean **COMPASSION OR ANGER OR BOTH,** and indeed in the incident of the healing of the leper (Mark 1:41) most Bible scholars believe Jesus was moved with anger at the leprosy, but of course anger and compassion can be experienced side by side in the human heart, and in Jesus' case anger at the work of satan and his evil spirits would also produce compassion for those who had suffered at their hands.

So then, allowing for righteous anger in Jesus at the sight of the crowds of sufferers with no one to turn to for help, I don't think anyone will quibble with acknowledging a sense of COMPASSION in the passage.

How does this Word affect us? Ask yourself the question, for which ministry does the Lord Jesus want, indeed, command us to pray to Him to raise up workers? Is it:

176

(1) teaching in our churches?
(2) proclaiming the gospel of the Kingdom?
(3) casting out demons?
(4) healing the sick?

How many of these ministries are YOU praying for?

Surely the passage demands that workers be sent out for ALL FOUR MINISTRIES, and NOT to pray for ALL FOUR is to disobey the imperative command of the Lord - **"(YOU) PRAY** therefore the Lord of the harvest...."

The deliverance ministry is described by Jesus as BREAD for the people of God (Matt. 15:26) and is perhaps the most dramatic and obvious manifestation of the compassion of the Lord Jesus Christ for the sea of suffering humanity around us. It **SHOWS** that God cares, really cares, and why the Lord Jesus *"went about doing good and curing all that were oppressed by the devil"* (Acts 10:38) It shows that *"the reason the Son of God was manifested was to LOOSE the works of the devil".* (1 John 3:8)

Answer this question please. How many churches do you know which are praying to the Lord of the Harvest to raise up labourers to cast out demons? And flowing from this is it not true to say that not only is the Bride of Christ disobedient in this important ministry of salvation, not only is she not ready for the Bridegroom but **she has not even seriously begun to pray in a way that will set in motion the vital stages of her preparation?**

Thank God for the Holy Spirit (Toronto Blessing) Revival!

10.3 IN ANSWER TO OUR PRAYERS

The reason that the Deliverance ministry is with us today

is that, whether we have known it or not, we have been praying for it whenever we have prayed the Lord's Prayer. The Lord's Prayer encourages us to pray **"deliver us from the evil one"** and **"Thy Kingdom come.** Thy will be done on earth, as it is in Heaven." These prayers are being answered now and will be answered in the future in a measure far beyond our past anticipations. Are you ready for the Lord to shake the Heaven and the earth (Heb. 12:25-29)? This will surely include us all because there is only one other place you could be, and you would not want to be THERE! Some folk think it is early days yet, but many Christians believe this shaking has already begun and it is much later on God's time-table than most of us realise.

10.4 PREPARATION OF THE BRIDE

The Kingdom of God IS NEAR AT HAND (Mark 1:15) and has come upon us (Matt. 12:28) and is in our midst (Luke 17:21) to warn us of the coming close of the Age (Matt. 28:20).

This ministry of deliverance demonstrated the Kingdom at the commencement of the New Testament age of the Spirit in Apostolic days and is now being restored to the church as this age now draws to a close with Christ's imminent return (Acts 2:19-20). **Prior to Christ's return and the restoration of all things, much of what the Old Testament prophets spoke must be fulfilled (Acts 3:20-25),** and I take this to essentially mean the cleansing of the temple (church) (1 Cor. 3:16, 2 Cor. 6:16 - 7:1) by deliverance. The cleansing and preparation of the Bride (church) is by deliverance (Eph. 5:26-27) because deliverance is an essential washing-by-word ministry. In other words, I understand Christ to be coming for a beautiful, cleansed, spirit-filled (plenty of oil in her lamp) Bride, **not**

178

a witchcraft-ridden, tradition-filled, useless old hag - divided, diseased and demonised. She will not only have the imputed righteousness and clothing of Christ UPON her, but she will be beautiful in her inward parts, because the Spirit of Christ FILLS her from within, and no unclean thing shall dwell within her.[1]

Thus I suggest that demons cast out of people should not be permitted to re-enter Christians. The result? The fully committed Christians will get cleaner and the pagans and the harlot church become even more unclean. The chasm between the true Church and the State will widen dramatically and God's people will indeed be Holy and separated from the rest of the world for God's purposes. (cf. John 15:18-19 etc.)

The stage will then be set for the Great Tribulation, and when the cleansed, true Church is raptured the world will be left with demonised hordes to face the judgement and wrath of God. **Thus deliverance IS a vital salvation ministry in our day and its restoration to the Christian church is no accident or peripheral matter** but lies at the heart of God's great salvation ready to be revealed in the last time (1 Peter 1:5). This is a wonderful purpose of the ministry of deliverance, i.e., **the complete RESTORATION of God's people from head to toe as needed by Job (Job 2:7), inside and outside, into the likeness of the Son of God![2] (Rom. 8:29, 2 Cor. 3:18)**

In conclusion I have put forward four (4) purposes for the Deliverance ministry in our day:

---

[1] Fully discussed in **"End-Time Deliverance and the Holy Spirit Revival"**.
[2] Fully discussed in **"End-Time Deliverance and the Holy Spirit Revival"**, also **"Your Full Salvation"**.

(1) **Evidence for the Kingdom or Rule of God.**
(2) **To set the captives free (i.e., the Lord's compassion).**
(3) **In answer to our prayers.**
(4) **Preparation of the Bride.**

All of these reasons are very good reasons in their own right for the ministry, but what emphasis, if any, should you and I have today? It has been said in church circles that so often the best is sacrificed for the good. What then is the BEST reason for the ministry? Notwithstanding that the above reasons overlap considerably, if you were obliged to choose ONE primary purpose, which would YOU consider as top priority? Your answer to this question will determine your application of the ministry.

Demonstrations of the Kingdom of God by signs and wonders during evangelistic crusades are great PROVIDED they are seen as a beginning, a pointer towards the TOTAL restoration job that the Lord wants to do in each precious child of God, and not seen simply as aids to evangelism, and therefore as an end in themselves. If they ARE seen as an end in themselves then the healing or deliverance signs or wonders may not last a month!

Yes, the prayer *"deliver us from the evil one"* has a broader and greater meaning than we normally understand and yes, the Lord answers prayers even when we ask Him things about which we know very little.

Yes, the Lord cares - He really does. The Word of God is true. HE IS LORD and His compassion knows no limits to those who call upon His Name. Indeed compassion is never far removed from the Lord's purposes but is inherent in every grace or miracle, and it is great to know that our prayers are truly answered more abundantly than we could ever think possible (Eph. 3:20). However, good as these reasons are, for me the top priority, and I believe it is the Lord's top priority, is the preparation of the Bride for His Son's Wedding Day! I would not argue with anyone who sought to fulfill all four purposes for the Deliverance ministry so long as the Bride's preparation, that is, her TOTAL cleansing and restoration, was not neglected.

You will gather from this that whereas PARTICULAR (or SPECIAL) deliverance (cleansing) for observably troubled Christians is fine, I believe that the WILL OF GOD TODAY is for TOTAL CLEANSING AND RESTORATION for every Christian, and that THIS is the Great Salvation ready to be revealed in the last days (1 Peter 1:5). This subject is so important for Christians today that we have published **"End-Time Deliverance"**[1] to explore and explain this Vision. I do hope you are able to get a copy.

---

[1] The 3rd edition of this book has been entitled **"End-Time Deliverance and the Holy Spirit Revival"** to accommodate the "Toronto Blessing."

EPILOG

In the next book (Book 4) I want to share the impact of the ministry of deliverance upon the way I now see the spiritual warfare. It has considerable biblical and discernment material, the kind of revelational material I could never have shared without first publishing Books 1, 2 and now 3, because I do not think that even many Christians in the Renewal movement would have been able to receive it without first weighing the evidence already presented.

I have called it **"Discerning Human Nature",** because that is what it is about, but even though it is like opening a can of worms, I trust it will be a very positive contribution to the preparation of the Bride, and to each one of us as individual members of the Bride that has made herself ready.

I am excited about Book 4 and if you have stuck with me this far you will know that there is no deceit or salesmanship polluting my words when I say to you to make sure you get or borrow a copy. I believe that for many it will be the most penetrating book, outside of the Bible, they have ever read.

May the Lord richly bless you as you catch the Vision He is giving the Bride, for Herself.

PETER HOBSON
CROWS NEST
SEPT. 1996

APPENDIX J

RESTORATION SCRIPTURES

1. "We (Christians)," Paul wrote, "ARE BEING CHANGED into His likeness (image) from glory into glory..." (2 Cor. 3:18).

2. **"LET US CLEANSE OURSELVES FROM ALL POL-LUTION of flesh and of spirit, perfecting holiness (separation for God's purposes) in the fear of God." (2 Cor. 7:1).**

3. "You sinners cleanse your hands (from evil deeds) and PURIFY YOUR HEARTS, you that are double-minded (two-souled)". (James 4:8).

4. "If therefore anyone CLEANSES himself, he will be a sanctified vessel for honour ... Flee youthful lusts, and pursue righteousness, faith, love, peace with those who call on the Lord out of a PURE HEART." (2 Tim. 2:21-22).

5. "Beloved, now we are children of God and it has not yet been shown what we shall be. We know that when He (Jesus) is manifested WE SHALL BE LIKE HIM, because we shall see Him as He is.

    And EVERYONE having this hope concerning Him PU-RIFIES HIMSELF as He is pure". (1 John 3:2-3).

6. "Many will be purged, purified (made white) and re-fined, but the wicked will act wickedly, and none of the

wicked will understand—but those who have ins[...]
will understand." (Dan. 12:10 N.A.S. Bible).

7. It is written of **John the Baptist** that:

    ...he came into all the district around the Jordan,
    preaching a baptism of repentance for forgiveness of
    sins; as it is written in the book of the words of Isaiah
    the prophet, "The voice of one crying in the wilder-
    ness,

    > 'MAKE READY THE WAY OF THE LORD. MAKE
    > HIS PATHS STRAIGHT. EVERY RAVINE SHALL
    > BE FILLED UP, AND EVERY MOUNTAIN AND
    > HILL SHALL BE BROUGHT LOW; AND THE
    > CROOKED SHALL BECOME STRAIGHT, AND
    > THE ROUGH ROADS SMOOTH; AND ALL
    > FLESH SHALL SEE THE SALVATION OF GOD.'"

    He therefore said to the multitudes who were going
    out to be baptized by him, "You brood of vipers, who
    warned you to flee from the wrath to come?

    "Therefore bring forth fruits in keeping with your repent-
    ance, and do not begin to say to yourselves, 'We have
    Abraham for our father,' for I say to you that God is able
    from these stones to raise up children to Abraham.

    "And also the axe is already laid at the root of the trees;
    every tree therefore that does not bear good fruit is cut
    down and thrown into the fire." (Luke 3:4-9)

Please note, an explanation in full of these scriptures is
made in **"Guidance for Those Receiving Deliverance."**

APPENDIX K

CONFESSION OF FAITH

.₃ Confession of Faith acknowledges its debt to **Rev. Dr John Osteen's** excellent "Confession" in his book **"There is a Miracle in Your Mouth".** We have simply fine-tuned it a little to apply more pointedly to the issues facing those in a Deliverance and Restoration program.

It is vital to remember that such a Confession expresses **positional, legal truths** expressed in the Word of God. It is as positional truth is expressed and believed by faith (Heb. 11:1) BY THOSE WHO ARE RECEIVING THE AP-PROPRIATE MINISTRY AND ARE ALSO IN THE CENTRE OF GOD'S WILL, that the legal position overtakes and over-comes our circumstances, and becomes REAL (Mark 11:22-24). Praise His Holy Name!

A GOOD DAILY CONFESSION

(i) FOUNDATION (Romans 10:9-10).

I confess with my mouth the Lord Jesus Christ and believe in my heart that God raised Him from the dead, THEREFORE I AM SAVED.

(ii) NEW CREATURE/LIFE

"If any man be in Christ he is a new creature. Old things have passed away and behold all things have become new." I am in Christ. I am a NEW CREATURE! I have a Father in heaven! I have life - everlasting life! I have a citizenship which is in heaven! I have a new realm in the Kingdom of God. I have been delivered out of the power of darkness and translated into the kingdom of God's dear Son! I am accepted in the BE-LOVED! My name is written in the Lamb's book of Life!

(iii) AUTHORITY

I HAVE AUTHORITY by the Word of God to tread on serpents and scorpions and over ALL THE POWER of the enemy AND NOTHING SHALL BY ANY MEANS HURT ME! I have authority over all demons to cast them out! I can lay hands on the sick and they shall recover! I am more than a conqueror through Jesus Christ. I can do all things through Christ who strengthens me to do His will.

(iv) BENEFITS OF THE CROSS

I confess the many benefits of the blood sacrifice of the Son of God.

Bless the Lord O my soul and forget not all His BEN-EFITS. Who forgives ALL my iniquities; who heals ALL my diseases. Who redeems my life from destruction. Who crowns me with loving kindness and tender mercy; who satisfies my mouth with good things that my strength is renewed. All my sins are forgiven! All my diseases are healed! My life is preserved and strong in God! I am crowned with His mercy!

(v) PROTECTION AND SALVATION

I confess I am not afraid!
Though I walk through the valley of the shadow of death I WILL FEAR NO EVIL! I FEAR NOT for you are WITH ME. I am not dismayed for you are my God. You are my HELP! You are my STRENGTH! You UP-HOLD me with the right hand of your righteousness!

186

You have not given me the spirit of fear, but of power, love and a sound mind. I have the SPIRIT OF POWER, LOVE and a SOUND MIND in me! (2 Tim. 1:7).

OVER me is the BLOOD OF THE LAMB! The Lord goes BEFORE me! Jesus is IN me! The angel of the Lord encamps AROUND me! UNDERNEATH me are the everlasting arms of God! Goodness and mercy FOLLOW me all the days of my life! Hallelujah!.... FEAR HAS NO PLACE IN MY LIFE! (John 10:4, John 14:20, Rom. 8:9, Ps. 34:7, Deut. 33:27, Ps. 23:6).

(vi) TODAY

I confess that this is a good day because the Lord made it for me to rejoice in!

I am delivered, healed, cleansed and restored today. I am filled with the love of God today. I am filled with the joy of the Lord TODAY! I am filled with the peace of God today. I am filled with the wisdom of God today. I am filled with the Holy Spirit today. These are mine TODAY!

I confess TODAY I will seek to help someone find the grace and mercy of God. I will rejoice today that heaven is my home. I will rejoice today that all my family are coming into the fold of the Lord! (2 Cor. 6:2).

(vii) SUMMARY

This is my confession. I boldly say it in front of God my Father, the Lord Jesus, the angels of God, and the devil and his angels. I thank you, Father, in Jesus' name, that I HAVE WHAT I SAY! MY CONFESSION RISES BEFORE YOU BASED UPON YOUR WORD! Jesus is the High Priest of my confession. He makes it good TODAY.

APPENDIX L

RENUNCIATION

When we are made aware of any iniquity or sin in our lives, we should at once **Confess, Renounce** and **Repent** of it, for we do not know if we shall be alive the next minute, nor do we know when the Lord will come from Heaven to catch up to Himself the dead in Christ, and us too, if we are His and are looking for His Appearing. We must be ready to appear before the judgement seat of Christ, for our rewards (1 Corinthians 3 v 11-15).

To C.R. and R. the following prayer may be helpful:

"Almighty God, I come to You in the Name of Jesus Christ and I confess the sin of _____ and renounce the sin of _____ and I repent of the sin of _____. I take away the ground I gave to the enemy, and I give it instead to my Lord Jesus Christ, and plead His Shed Blood to cleanse me from this sin. Thank you Father for forgiving me because of Jesus' Blood. Thank you Jesus for dying for me."

Praise your Holy Name!
Amen!

*We acknowledge the source of this prayer format as **"The Deliverer",** the official newsletter of **Norwood Christian Fellowship, London, England.***

APPENDIX M

THE CHRISTIAN ARMOUR

Be sprinkled with the **Blood of Jesus.**
>>> 1 Peter 1:2, Rom. 3:25. (NKJV)

Be clothed with the **armour of light.**
>>> Rom. 13:8.

Be clothed with the **Lord Jesus Christ.**
>>> Rom. 13:14. Gal. 3:27.

Be clothed with a **gentle and a quiet spirit.**
>>> 1 Peter 3:3.

Be clothed with **Power.**
>>> Luke 24:49.

Be clothed with the breastplate of **faith and love.**
>>> 1 Thess. 5:8.

Be clothed with **humility** toward one another.
>>> 1 Peter 5:5.

Be clothed with **the whole armour of God:**

   gird your loins with truth,

   put on the breastplate of righteousness,

   shod your feet with the preparation of the gospel of peace

   take the shield of faith,

   take the helmet of salvation,

   take the sword of the Spirit of the Word,

   pray with the Spirit at all times,

   keep watch with all perserverance - Eph. 6:10-18.

Don't worry about worldly clothing: 1 Peter 3:3, Matt. 6:25

The apostle Paul tells us to use the members of our bodies as weapons of righteousness:

"Therefore do not let sin reign (as a king) in your mortal body for the purpose of obeying its lusts.

Neither present your members to sin as weapons of un-righteousness, but present yourselves to God as those who have been brought from the dead to the living, and your members to God as **WEAPONS OF RIGHTEOUSNESS".** *(Romans 6:12-13)*

190

TRADE ENQUIRIES

PHILIPPINES

The Good News of Jesus
Christ Fellowship Inc.
P.O Box 6
CAGAYAN DE ORO CITY
9000 PHILIPPINES

U. S. A.

Impact Christian Books, Inc.
332 Leffingwell Ave, Suite 101
Kirkwood
Mo 63122
U. S. A.

Tel: (314) 822 3309
Fax: (314) 822 3325

UNITED KINGDOM

Sword Publications
P.O. Box 139
Aberdeen AB9 8LF
SCOTLAND

Tel: (1224) 480 294
Fax: (1224) 312 727

AFRICA

SJBS Outreach Inc.
P.O. Box 4953 Oshodi
Lagos, NIGERIA
WEST AFRICA

Full Salvation Ministry
P.O. Box 3438 KISII
KENYA, E.AFRICA

Tel: 381 31319

AUSTRALIA

W.A. Buchanan and Co.,
20 Morrisby St.,
(P.O. Box 206)
GEEBUNG, QLD., 4034

Tel: (07) 3865 2600   Fax: (07) 3865 2222

MINISTRY ENQUIRES TO:

Full Salvation Fellowship Ltd.
P. O. Box 1020
Crows Nest, 2065
AUSTRALIA

Tel: (02) 9436 3657   Fax: (02) 9437 6700

This book is produced by **FULL SALVATION FELLOWSHIP** and is designed to assist the people of God in their preparation for the drama of the End Time, which we believe has already begun on God's calendar.

The others published are:

"Guidance For Those Receiving Deliverance" (the old title of this was "So Now You Are Receiving Deliverance")

"Sex, Demons and Morality"

"The Reincarnation Deception"

"Toronto and the Truths You Need to Know"

"Your Full Salvation"

"Christian Authority and Power"

"Surviving the Distress of Nations"

"End-Time Deliverance and the Holy Spirit Revival"

"Head Covering and Lady Pastor - Teachers"

Christian Deliverance Book 1 - **"Make Yourselves Ready"**

Christian Deliverance Book 2 - **"Engaging the Enemy"**

Others in the process of production and to be published soon are:

Christian Deliverance Book 4 - **"Discerning Human Nature"**

"The Stigmata of Jesus"

CʒꙄꙄ ✿ CʒꙄꙄ

MORE COMMENTS

Recently I have come across your edifying book "Walking in Victory - Book 3" which is very impressive and instructive for ministry.

S.T. Ratnaswamy, Elder
New Bombay, INDIA.

My heartfelt thanks and gratitude, for through your deliverance series books my mind was opened . . .

Rev. Marciano A. Pandalan
Wharf Bible Study Centre
Pagadian, PHILIPPINES.

I have seen your books on spiritual warfare (1, 2 and 3) and they are very good indeed.

Alan Lee, Dublin,
REPUBLIC OF IRELAND.

I have just read with great interest and increasing excitement your books on Christian Deliverance (the first three volumes . . .) . . . your books speak to us powerfully.

Doug Smart
London, ENGLAND.

I have been blessed with your publications and encourage you to continue to do all that you can to open the eyes of the sleeping Church and urge them to get set free, committed and obedient to the word of God or in time they will fall away . . . your words are true . . . (do) not stop at any cost!

David Kriss (Jewish prophet)
Nth Balwyn, Vic. AUST.

We thank you so much for the Book 3 "Walking in Victory". It was so wonderful to be led by the Lord to buy it. It was at the right time the Lord gave us the right book which really inspired and encouraged us.

Rev. C. Robertnathaniel
Sanathnagar Hyderabad,
INDIA.

"Walking in Victory" (Book 3) – it's really restored by spiritual life and touch me my heart. Please send your books to help establish a Bible School in my country (Burma) . . .

Philip V. L. Thanga
Reading for Bachelor of Divinity
Immanuel Theological Seminary
New Delhi INDIA.